ROBINSON COLLEGE CHAPEL

Hearing the Other

Inclusive Liturgy at Robinson College

Contents

IV PRAYERS OF INTERCESSION

Preface

*'I am the way, the truth, and the life. No one comes to
the Father, except by me.'*
  (John 14:6)

Robinson College Chapel has championed inclusivity since long
before inclusivity became the cardinal virtue. According to the
author of John's Gospel, the words cited above were uttered by
Jesus and they sound pretty 'exclusive'. In this light, a phrase
like 'inclusive liturgy' might sound self-contradictory. Liturgy
is a word usually used of Christian worship, and there is a
widespread assumption that you cannot be both committed to
a particular belief system (such as Christianity), and inclusive
(ready to accommodate alternatives). On the surface then,
'inclusive liturgy' is an oxymoron. It is delusional, impossible,
pointless.

Such an assumption, however, is rooted in a self-aggrandizing
belief-system of its own, namely that of 'modernity'. In
modernity, it was possible for the enlightened individual to
scale the heights of Mount Olympus and gaze down upon lesser
mortals. From the Olympian heights, we would be free of all
ideology, free of all delusion and subjectivity, free of all context.
A pure, objective view of the world as it really is. Unfortunately,
any who did make it to the summit discovered that Olympus is

the home of many gods. Not one of them was free of delusion, subjectivity, prejudice, assumption or bias. So where does that leave us?

Every human, every community, every system of belief or non-belief, has a context of its own. After all, 'a text without a context is a con'. No, the only position from which a person or a community can be genuinely inclusive, is a position of commitment to something. Otherwise, there is nothing in which the outsider can be included 'into'. Inclusivity, in sum, requires a commitment, a community, and a context.

The context of Robinson College has long been unusual amongst Cambridge Colleges. Since its foundation, the Chapel has been 'ecumenical'. With very few exceptions, the Colleges of both Oxford and Cambridge are Anglican foundations, Chapels that come under the remit of the Church of England. Robinson is one of only two ecumenical Chapels (the other, being at Fitzwilliam College). Ecumenical is, in essence, a Christian term for inclusivity. It refers to the entire 'household' of God's people, a tradition that seeks to welcome folk from other Christian traditions without seeking to replace any particular form or worship, or convert any who attend.

These attempts at inclusivity have always marked the liturgies, that is the forms of worship, that we have chosen as a Chapel community. In more recent parlance, ecumenical has also come to refer to a sensitivity and openness shown to non-Christian traditions.

Of course, our Chapel community belongs not only to a Christian tradition, but also to a choral tradition rooted in institutional Christian belief. Our Chapel Choir includes people from many backgrounds, religious and non-religious. All choirs in such a tradition necessarily perform music that is often centuries old. This means that some of the language and belief may seem very dated, and is used today with the assumption that those attending will understand the historical context in which this music was composed.

Nevertheless, our community has always sought to show sensitivity in its language and ethos, an approach modelled by our first Chaplain, Rev. Dr David Stacey, and replicated by his successors. Today, the challenges we face are largely concerned with ethics and language, so it is important to address the use of some of the language adopted throughout the orders of worship offered in this book.

Lord: Originally, Jewish worshippers of God dared not even utter a name for him/her because to do so is already to assume a familiarity, to domesticate the Other, to bring this unnamed something under human control. In the Bible, the word LORD (in capital letters) is used to highlight this unknown-ness of God's name (traditionally expressed as YHWH/Yahweh). The name, Jehovah is the result of post-biblical attempts at mixing the letters from YHWH with the vowels from the word Adonai (the Jewish term for 'Lord'). In its Anglo-Saxon origins, the Lord was literally, the Loaf-Ward – the individual whose authority was used to ensure that his people were cared for. When used in the liturgies below, it is intended to be understood primarily in this sense, namely authority granted to ensure the welfare of others.

Father: Perhaps the most problematic element of Christian worship today is the use of gender exclusive language. This, of course, is partly historical accident, since many ancient societies were exclusively patriarchal. This was profoundly true of the Roman Empire that ruled the territories where the historical Jesus lived out his entire life. The rights of every father were enshrined in law, from the marble corridors of power to the flea-ridden provinces of conquered territories. At the top of this patriarchy, was the Roman emperor itself. In this light, it may well be that by using the word 'Father' to address God directly (rather than appealing for justice through the hierarchical chain of father's around which the empire was structured), Jesus was being deliberately subversive. His use of the word 'Father' may thus have undermined the all-pervasive patriarchy of his day.

Kingdom: The Kingdom of God has long been taken to refer to heaven, the final resting place of the tediously well-behaved. For some, it refers to the so-called 'Second Coming' when – as some Christians believe, Jesus of Nazareth will return from heaven to draw human history to a close. For others still, it refers to the peoples and individuals conquered by Christian belief. However, in its origins kingdom referred to the reign rather than the realm of the a king. In other words, it refers to a form of authority at odds with the power games of measurable human powers based on financial strength, military might, or public relations. Jesus offered a radically alternative power dynamic, and that is what was originally meant by the word Kingdom. When Jesus called his followers to pray, 'thy kingdom come', he was telling them to pray for regime change.

Sin and Forgiveness: Sin is widely deemed a convenient tool for controlling the mindless masses of the Christian era. It refers to those elements of human behaviour that do not reflect the nature of the God they claim to worship. For this reason, in order to guarantee a place in the afterlife, and to ensure God does not unexpectedly grant you early access, sin has to be forgiven – otherwise God will be angry and you will spend eternity being punished. In its ancient origins, sin referred first and foremost to debt. Forgiveness referred to debt cancellation. These elements of sin and forgiveness cannot and should not be excluded from whatever metaphorical uses these words may later have been put to.

Confession: Similarly, confession is often deemed to be the means by which Christians '-fess up', own up to the terrible sins they have committed, so that God, in turn, will forgive them. This conviction still finds its way into most liturgies. However, confession originally meant simply speaking with integrity, 'saying the same thing', so that our lips and our lives are in harmony. Confession then, as understood in the liturgies of this book, is used to encourage worshippers to face the truth about themselves and their place in the world. It is in so doing, that worshippers might grow in their own self-awareness, and awareness of the world around them.

Holiness: Widely mistaken as just another word for piety, righteousness or purity, holiness is often viewed in very negative terms. Hence the phrase, 'holier than thou.' And yet, it denotes that which is set apart, different, separate. A major element of this idea, would be expressed today with the word, Otherness. In a positive sense, the Other – or in biblical terms – the Holy, is that which stands over against us. It is the being or the reality that threatens our assumptions, undermines our knowledge, and hangs the question mark of doubt over all our certainties. The Other, in this sense, can be both a threat to our current mindset and an invitation to inhabit a new mindset. It is precisely that shift in mindset that the bible describes using the word, *repentance.*

Sermons: Jesus of Nazareth never once 'preached', nor did he ever give a 'sermon'. Such a practice seems to refer to little more than pious individuals with over-inflated self-opinions delivering belittling advice based on iron-age mythologies. For this reason, the talks heard in our Chapel are not referred to as 'sermons'. Jesus himself delivered prophecies. These were not necessarily supernaturally granted predictions of the future, but much closer to the practice today known as 'speaking truth to power'. When addressing his fellows, Jesus sought to initiate a change in mind set. Since minds are not easily changed, the goal of those invited to speak in Chapel, is to evoke the reaction, 'that made me think.' Since thinking involved the mind, the heart, the bowels, the genitals, and entails our past and future, along with our self-understanding, encouraging people to think is no easy task. It is our hope that those invited to address the congregation of Robinson Chapel will seek to do just that.

Intercessions: Prayer takes various forms, one of which is 'prayers for the world', also known as 'intercession'. Traditionally, the role of the 'priest' would be as a broker between God and the world. Praying would be representing the people to God, Preaching would be representing God to the people. Several traditions, however, adopt belief in the 'priesthood of all believers'. This does not mean so much, that every individual is their own priest. Rather that, the gathered community as a whole has a priestly function of representing God to the people, and the people to God. Several Christian traditions today have ceased to include prayers of intercession (i.e., prayers for anyone other than those present in church), because they 'interrupt the flow of worship'. Other traditions often seem to pray dispassionately for the world, as though waving a liturgical wand over the headlines of world news, and asking God to fix everything. At Robinson, our hope is to pray in such a way as to feel the plight of those for whom we pray, commit ourselves where possible to make their plight known, and to offer ourselves as a means by which such prayer might be answered.

The Lord's Prayer: The prayer that Jesus taught his followers, known as the Lord's Prayer, includes many of the elements of worship outlined above. The present book has four separate translations of this prayer. Two of these are simply translation from one language into another, and may sound familiar even to folk who rarely attend church. Two are translated also into our host culture, taking into account some of the elements of worship outlined above. Historically, it is likely that this prayer also served as a *creed*, an identity marker outlining the ethical stance to which the followers of Jesus might be held accountable. This book includes little in the way of creeds, partly because of the problematic nature of their history, partly because of their exclusivity, but mainly because the Lord's Prayer fulfils all the functions of a creed, and more.

Part of a biblical understanding of humanity, is that humans are created to live in community, persons-in-relationship rather than individuals-in-isolation. A widespread practice of welcoming the stranger, the alien, the outsider, was commonplace in many ancient middle eastern societies, and this is reflected in the writings of Jewish and Christian Scriptures. But no community can model this to everyone's satisfaction. The church's mistakes, hypocrisies and delusions have long been well publicised. In contemporary society, much has yet to be learned about secular shortcomings in the practice of inclusivity: the selective solidarity that often will speak on behalf of those we might be too afraid to listen to in real life; the delusional diversities that still unwittingly favour 'people like me'; and the image-only inclusivity, that continues to exclude people on the basis of age, class, and religious belief. Regardless of our background and convictions, regardless of our belief or non-belief, surely it's possible that we can always do better.

The liturgy offered in this book, it is hoped, both recognises our perpetual human failures, but also presents a means by which we encourage and challenge one another into listening well to the Other. Our current practice is far less important than our active relationship with those who disagree, those who are 'outside', and who challenge us. It is from such folk we are likely to hear the truth about who we really are, and it is among such folk that the Jesus worshipped here made and makes himself thoroughly at home.

Simon Perry, Michaelmas 2023

I

Ecumenical Orders of Service

1

A First Order for Evening Worship

¶ *All stand at the entrance of the choir*

CALL TO WORSHIP

Your word is a light to our feet
And a light upon our path

HYMN (see boards for hymn numbers)

¶ *Remain standing*

Let us praise God,
The Lord of time and space, born into a feeding trough.
All hearts are open before you.
Worshipped by leaders, by citizens, by asylum-seekers.
All people are equal before you.
Who humbles those who strut the corridors of power, and
exalts those who limp through the jungle of the refugee camp.
All motives are laid bare before you.

God of all life and of each life.
All are as one before you.

We bring before you all our pride and all our shame, all our success and all our failure, all our hope and all our anxiety, our knowledge and our ignorance, our gratitude and our frustration, our past and our future.
All hearts are open before you.
And we praise you.

¶ *All sit*

ADORATION AND CONFESSION

Loving God, who meets us in the name of Emmanuel.
We praise you.
May we encounter you in one another
We worship you.
May we see your face in one another
We listen for you.
May we hear your voice from one another.
Help us to become your gift to others, to receive your grace from others, and to be remade by our encounter with others.
Forgive us when we have failed one another, and so failed you.
Help us to forgive when others have wronged us.
Show us how to live together in all the failure and the friction, in all the grace and the goodness of human community. And so, may we receive ourselves back from one another, transformed ever more fully into your likeness.
Amen.

WELCOME AND NOTICES

A HYMN or CHOIR ANTHEM

LISTENING FOR THE OTHER

THE FIRST READING:
    "Listen now for the word of God, through ..."
    At the end: "Thanks be to God." **Amen**

HYMN

THE SECOND READING:
    "Listen now for the word of God, through ..."
    At the end: "Thanks be to God." **Amen**

THE ADDRESS

RESPONSE

CHOIR ANTHEM

PRAYERS FOR THE WORLD

At the end,
    God of authority, God of care,
    God of Justice, power and love.
    Make yourself known
    in the outcast and the other.
    Let your regime of justice come,
    And let your holy will be done, in action as it is in intent.

May we share the plight of those in need,
Until their need becomes our own.
Then give us this day, enough for this day.
Wipe our slates clean,
As we clean the slate of the debts due to us.
Do not lead us into hardship,
But keep us free from oppression and evil.
Because this is your kingdom, your power, your glory.
Both now and forever. Let it be so.

DISMISSAL

HYMN

¶ *Remain standing*

May the LORD bless you and keep you. The LORD make his face to shine upon you and be gracious to you. The LORD lift up the light of his countenance upon you, and give you peace. **Amen.**

THE CHOIR SINGS A FINAL AMEN

¶ *Please remain seated for the organ voluntary. The Warden leaves first, followed by fellows.*

2

A Second Order for Evening Worship

¶ *All stand at the entrance of the choir*

GATHERING WITH ONE ANOTHER

We gather to encounter one another:
To hear words that challenge and affirm us.
To hear voices past and present.
To listen and think, and become more fully ourselves.
To encounter the Other.
To give thanks for this day and this community.
To give thanks for our place within in it.

HYMN (see boards for hymn numbers)

¶ *Remain standing*

For the eons and the ages that brought this moment to be.
For every day already lived, and every day awaiting us,

For every split second and every heartbeat granted to us.
We praise you.

For the company and community, gathered here and now.
For the people and the thought and the experience, that carry us beyond ourselves.
For those who love us for who we are, and encourage us to be more,
We praise you.

For the privileges already enjoyed
For the opportunities that still await.
For the presence of others and the hope they bring.
We praise you.

¶ *All sit*

FACING TRUTH AND CELEBRATING LIFE

Let us face up to who we have been, and who we might become.

When we have wronged others.
May we find strength enough to face truth.
When others highlight our faults for us,
May we find courage enough to hear them.
When they are right,
May we find the confidence to accept it.
When our wrongs require action to make things right.
May we find courage enough to take it.

May our relationships be open and honest, that our growth may be real, and the life of the world be enriched.

And so, in one another's company, we celebrate gift of life.

All that is given to us.

 All that is asked of us.

 All that comforts and disturbs us.

 All that makes us who we are.

For a greater Other, that finds expression in one another,

 We seek to hear and respond.

WELCOME AND NOTICES

HYMN or CHOIR ANTHEM

HEARING THE OTHER

THE FIRST READING:

 "Listen now for the voice of the Other, through ..."

 At the end: "Thanks be to God." **Amen**

HYMN

THE SECOND READING:

 "Listen now for the voice of the Other, through ..."

 At the end: "Thanks be to God." **Amen**

THE ADDRESS

THE RESPONSE

CHOIR ANTHEM

PRAYERS FOR THE WORLD

At the end,

Mother and Father of All,
   Fountain of space and time,
   Your name is above and beyond,
   All we can know or achieve.
   May your justice be known here and now.
   May the highest hopes
   of outsiders and outcasts,
   be fulfilled here and now.
   Let the wealthy know hunger.
   Let the hungry know wealth.
   Free us from failure and shame,
   As we pardon those who have wronged us.
   And make us neither victims nor agents of evil.
   Because the kingdom, the power and the glory are yours,
   Now and forever.

GOING OUT

HYMN

¶ *Remain standing*

May the friendships fostered here, draw from and feed into something greater still.

May the truths heard here, draw our attention to something greater still.

May all that is celebrated here, spill into the world beyond this time and this place, and radiate something greater still.

THE CHOIR SINGS A FINAL AMEN

¶ *Please remain seated for the organ voluntary. The Warden leaves first, followed by fellows.*

3

A Third Order for Evening Worship

¶ *All stand at the entrance of the choir*

GATHERING

Look! God makes himself thoroughly at home with people.
 He will live with them, and they will be *his* people,
 And God himself will be with them,
 And he will be their God.

HYMN (see boards for hymn numbers)

¶ *Remain standing*

Loving God, we worship you as the Lord of space and time, who meets us here and now.

You are the God of creation
 Who brings something out of nothing.
 You are the God of salvation

Who brings hope out of failure.
You are the God of liberation
Who brings justice for those who have been denied it.

You are the Lord of Hosts
Who was born into an occupied territory.
You are the Lord of eternity,
Who became a peasant tradesman.
You are the Lord Almighty,
At home in the lowest echelons of society.
You are the Lord of heaven and earth,
Who became marginalised, outcast, excluded.
You are the Lord God,
whose power is expressed in powerlessness.

¶ *All sit*

CONFRONTING TRUTH

Almighty and everlasting God.
We praise you as the God who meets with us,
In all our frailty and failure.
Who rejoices with us,
In all our thankfulness and joy
Who celebrates with us,
In all our triumphs and gains.

So awaken us more fully to who we are,
Who we are to others and to you.
In your presence,
May our delusion meet reality.

May our pretension meet truth.
May our despair meet hope.

In your presence, we are reminded that
We have failed others, and in so doing, failed you.
Forgive us our debts.
We have turned a blind eye to those who needed our help.
Forgive us our debts.
We have thought and spoken wrongly of others.
Forgive us our debts.
We have chosen not to hear uncomfortable truth about the world,
and about our place in it.
Forgive us our debts.

Leave us not in debt to one another.
Restore our relationships with others.
Deepen our trust in them and in you.
For the sake of your name.
Amen.

WELCOME AND NOTICES

HYMN or CHOIR ANTHEM

COMMISSIONING

THE FIRST READING:
"Listen now for the word of God, through ..."
At the end: "Thanks be to God." **Amen**

HYMN

THE SECOND READING:
   "Listen now for the word of God, through ..."
   At the end: "Thanks be to God." **Amen**

THE ADDRESS

RESPONDING

CHOIR ANTHEM

PRAYERS FOR THE WORLD

At the end,
   Loving God in heaven, hallowed be your name,
   Your kingdom come,
   Your will be done on earth as in heaven.
   Give us today our daily bread.
   Forgive us our sins as we forgive those who sin against us.
   Lead us not into temptation but deliver us from evil,
   For the kingdom, the power and the glory are yours,
   Now and evermore. Amen.

SENDING OUT

HYMN

¶ *Remain standing*

God of creation
Make us bearers of your image.
Spirit of Community
Make us hearers of your word,
Son of righteousness,
Make us agents of your justice.
God the three-in-one
Make us channels of your love.

THE CHOIR SINGS A FINAL AMEN

¶ *Please remain seated for the organ voluntary. The Warden leaves first, followed by fellows.*

4

A Fourth Order for Evening Worship

¶ *All stand at the entrance of the choir*

THE CALL TO WORSHIP

O Lord, open our lips,
And our mouths will proclaim your praise.

HYMN (see boards for hymn numbers)

¶ *Remain standing*
We worship you as Father, Son and Holy Spirit, the God who lives and moves and has his being in self-giving relationship, the God who is love. And so, God of Love, as you invite us into your presence, we bring all that we are.

Our success and our failure,
Our triumphs and our wounds.
You welcome us as we are.

Our gifts and our limitations,
Our strength and our vulnerability.
You welcome us as we are.

Our expectation and our despair,
Our joy and our sadness.
You welcome us as we are.

We praise you that, in your presence, we learn who we are.
And we praise you that you do not leave us as we are.
Amen.

¶ *All sit*

ADORATION AND CONFESSION

As we seek to grow in our relationship to others and to you
Help us to face up to who we are.

We are truly sorry for those times when we have been less than
ourselves.
When we have hurt others, and think they deserved it.
When we have hurt others, without knowing.
When we have hurt others, and did not care.

We are truly sorry for those times when we have been agents of
injustice.
When ignorance has been too blissful, and truth too painful.
When we have revelled in the rightness of our own cause, and
the wrongness of others.

When we have made mountains out of molehills, and trivialised major injustices.

God of love, God of justice, may we remain ever ready to change our minds and change our lives, to be transformed by our lives with others, to be remade by our encounter with you.
Amen.

WELCOME AND NOTICES

HYMN or CHOIR ANTHEM

MINISTRY OF THE WORD

THE FIRST READING:
"Listen now for the word of God, through ..."
At the end: "Thanks be to God." **Amen**

HYMN

THE SECOND READING:
"Listen now for the word of God, through ..."
At the end: "Thanks be to God." **Amen**

THE ADDRESS

THE RESPONSE

CHOIR ANTHEM

PRAYERS OF INTERCESSION

At the end,

God of authority, God of care,
God of Justice, power and love.
Make yourself known,
in the outcast and the other.
Let your regime of justice come,
And let your holy will be done, in action as it is in intent.
May we share the plight of those in need,
Until their need becomes our own.
Then give us this day, enough for this day.
Wipe our slates clean,
As we clean the slate of the debts due to us.
Do not lead us into hardship,
But keep us free from oppression and evil.
Because this is your kingdom, your power, your glory.
Both now and forever. Let it be so.

THE DISMISSAL

HYMN

¶ *Remain standing*

God the Parent of All, Spirit of Community, Word made flesh:

Fill us with your divine love,
Strengthen our commitment to one another,
Inspire us with the passion of Jesus,
Now and always.
Amen

THE CHOIR SINGS A FINAL AMEN

¶ *Please remain seated for the organ voluntary. The Warden leaves first, followed by fellows.*

5

A Fifth Order for Evening Worship

¶ *All stand at the entrance of the choir*

GATHERING WITH ONE ANOTHER

God of Abraham, Isaac, and Jacob,
God of Sarah and Rebekah, Leah and Rachel,
Creator of all, Lord of all, Strength and Hope of all,
We worship you with all that we are.
And praise you in all things.

HYMN (see boards for hymn numbers)

¶ *Remain standing*

God of loyalty, hope and love,
We praise you as Lord of all life and of each life,
We gather in the name of Jesus.

God of the ages, and God of the moment,
We gather to encounter you.
Spirit of silence, and the still small voice.
We gather to hear you speak.
Word made flesh, the friend of sinners,
We gather to meet with you.

Into your presence, we bring all that we are:
Our love and our cruelty,
Our passion and our apathy,
Our courage and our cowardice.

¶ *All sit*

FACING TRUTH AND CELEBRATING LIFE

God of grace, who heals wounds and restores relationships.
Help us to face up to our own faults.

We long to make the world a better place, without making ourselves better people.
We want to challenge others, and we don't anyone to challenge us.
We hunger and thirst justice, but we want it our way.
Show us the truth about ourselves.

We want to end poverty, but not enough to help its victims.
Only pray for them.
We want to welcome the Other, but not their Otherness.
Only their image.
We want the kingdom of God, but not its king.

23

Only his throne.
Show us the truth about ourselves.

Some conversation may be difficult, and we dare not have it.

Some action we are avoiding haunts our dreams, and we dare not take it.

Some words we regret require apology – but we dare not make it.

Give us courage to act.

Restore our relationships with others, and with you.

And may our lives draw attention to something greater than ourselves.

WELCOME AND NOTICES

HYMN or CHOIR ANTHEM

THE WORD

THE FIRST READING:
"Listen now for the word of God, through ..."
At the end: "Thanks be to God." **Amen**

HYMN

THE SECOND READING:
"Listen now for the word of God, through ..."
At the end: "Thanks be to God." **Amen**

THE ADDRESS

THE RESPONSE

CHOIR ANTHEM

PRAYERS FOR THE WORLD
   At the end,

Mother and Father of All,
   Fountain of space and time,
   Your name is above and beyond,
   All we can know or achieve.
   May your justice be known here and now.
   May the highest hopes
   of outsiders and outcasts,
   be fulfilled here and now.
   Let the wealthy know hunger.
   Let the hungry know wealth.
   Free us from failure and shame,
   As we pardon those who have wronged us.
   And make us neither victims nor agents of evil.
   Because the kingdom, the power and the glory are yours,
   Now and forever.
   Amen

SENDING OUT

HYMN

¶ *Remain standing*

25

God of evening and of morning
   God of all that has passed, and all that will,
   God of endings and new beginnings,
   We commit ourselves to your loving kindness.
   May others encounter your peace,
   Because you have granted it to us.
   Amen

THE CHOIR SINGS A FINAL AMEN

¶ *Please remain seated for the organ voluntary. The Warden leaves first, followed by fellows.*

6

A Sixth Order for Evening Worship

¶ *All stand at the entrance of the choir*

GATHERING

Hear, O Israel:
The LORD our God, the LORD is one.
And each one among you, shall love the LORD your God:
With all your heart, with all your being, with all your strength.

HYMN (see boards for hymn numbers)

¶ *Remain standing*

We worship you as Emmanuel, the God who is with us.
In all things, in every moment,
You are with us.
In our joy and in our sorrow,
You are with us.

In our arrogance and in our shame,
You are with us.
In our brokenness and in our strength,
You are with us.
In our ignorance and in our knowledge,
You are with us.
In Jesus Christ, the outcast, the Risen Lord.
You are with us, here and now.

¶ *All sit*

CONFRONTING TRUTH

We worship you as God of eternity, who meets us in this time and this place.

We worship you as God of creation, further away than the furthest galaxy, closer to us than we are to ourselves.

We worship you as God almighty, who welcomes us in our frailty and in our need.

We worship you as God of grace, who forgives and restores, who heals and remakes.

Forgive us now, we pray.

We have averted our gaze from suffering, and in so doing, averted it from you.

We have taken the path of least resistance, and convinced ourselves we were right.

We have rationalised poor decisions, choices made for reasons we dare not face.

We have closed our ears to those who expose our hypocrisy, and threaten our pretence.

We have claimed to be open minded, but failed to change our mindset when it mattered.

Forgive us we pray, change our minds, and change our lives.
Give us hope to displace our despair.
Give us courage to overcome our fear.
Give us compassion to counter our indifference.
To the glory of your name.
Amen.

WELCOME AND NOTICES

HYMN or CHOIR ANTHEM

COMMISSIONING

THE FIRST READING:
"Listen now for the word of God, through ..."
At the end: "Thanks be to God." **Amen**

HYMN

THE SECOND READING:
"Listen now for the word of God, through ..."
At the end: "Thanks be to God." **Amen**

THE ADDRESS

RESPONDING

CHOIR ANTHEM

PRAYERS FOR THE WORLD

At the end,

Loving God in heaven, hallowed be your name,
Your kingdom come,
Your will be done on earth as in heaven.
Give us today our daily bread.
Forgive us our sins as we forgive those who sin against us.
Lead us not into temptation but deliver us from evil,
For the kingdom, the power and the glory are yours,
Now and evermore. Amen.

SENDING OUT

HYMN

¶ *Remain standing*

Expect great things from God,
  Attempt great things for God,
  God be with us, now and always.

THE CHOIR SINGS A FINAL AMEN

¶ *Please remain seated for the organ voluntary. The Warden leaves first, followed by fellows.*

II

ALTERNATIVE COMMUNION SERVICES

7

A First Order for Choral Communion

¶ *All stand*

OPENING SENTENCE

HYMN (see boards for hymn numbers)

¶ *All sit*

God of every epoch, and every Galaxy.
    God of every split second and every square inch.
    Nothing is hidden from you, nothing beyond your knowledge.
    Confront us we pray, with your challenge and with your grace.
    With your expectation, and with your encouragement.
    Draw us into your being,
    Remake us in your image,
    Send us out into your world,
    That the lives entrusted to us,
    might serve to make you known.

Often, we sense our failure to make you known.

All too often, we do not.

When presented with your challenge,

We have taken the easy path.

When witnessing injustice,

We have turned a blind eye.

When challenged about our greed,

We have justified ourselves.

When faced by those who need our support,

We have busied ourselves elsewhere.

When confronted with our tribalism,

We have withdrawn to our peers.

May we be forgiven the wrongs we have done.

May we forgive others for wrongs done to us.

May we own our wrongdoing, in such a way as to learn.

So that our lives reflect your goodness.

Amen.

¶ *The choir may sing*

Kyrie eleison,

Christe eleison

Kyrie eleison.

Lord have mercy,

Christ have mercy,

Lord, have mercy.

¶ *All sit*

HYMN

READING
At the end
Thanks be to God

THE ADDRESS

PRAYERS FOR THE WORLD

Ending with
Mother and Father of All,
Fountain of space and time,
Your name is above and beyond,
All we can know or achieve.
May your justice be known here and now.
May the highest hopes of outsiders and outcasts,
find down to earth fulfilment.
Let the wealthy know hunger.
Let the hungry know wealth.
Free us from failure and shame,
As we pardon those who have wronged us.
And make us neither victims nor agents of evil.

THE GREAT THANKSGIVING

¶ *All stand*

The Lord be with you:
And also with you
Lift up your hearts:

We lift them to the Lord
Let us give thanks to the Lord our God:
It is right to give thanks and praise.

It is right and just, because you have made us, provided for us, and, enabled us to flourish, to fail and fail better, to learn and to grow, to love and be loved. The beauty we have witnessed, the good we have tasted, the love we have known, have their genesis in you. The support that has carried us, the grace that has touched us, the hope that has driven us, find their perfection in you.

And in Jesus we see hope fulfilled. We praise you for breaking into our human experience in the person of Jesus of Nazareth. We thank you for the directness of his speech, for the integrity of his life, for the courage of his convictions, for the risks he took, for the dangers he faced, for the justice he sought, for the sacrifice he made.

And we thank you for the Spirit by which he overcomes death. That same Spirit who awakens in us our compulsion to encounter this Jesus here and now, who draws us ever nearer to him, who binds us ever more fully to one another, who leads us to become more fully ourselves. And so, we add our own voices to the song of the Church on earth and in heaven:

¶ *The Choir may sing:*

Sanctus, Sanctus, Sanctus,
  Dominus Deus Sabaoth
  Pleni sunt coeli et terra gloria tua.
  Hosanna in excelsis.

36

Holy, holy, holy,
> **God of power and might,**
> **Heaven and earth are full of Thy glory.**
> **Hosanna in the highest.**

And so, since words both serve us and fail us, we fall silent and call to mind the Prophet, mighty in Word and Action. May his courage seep into our hearts. May his comfort rage through our spirit. May his call-to-action echo through our bones.

Silence

Spirit of mercy, kindness and love. Rest in our midst as we share this food and this drink. May this meal bring satisfaction and synergy, as together we receive and we share the welcome, the liberty, the renewal that Christ alone can bring.

¶ *All sit*

THE BREAKING OF THE BREAD

With friends around a table, an anxious young man lifted a chunk of bread, broke it, and said,
> "This is my body – broken for you."

Later, he lifted a cup of wine and said,
> "This is the new relationship with God, enabled by my death. Each of you should drink it to remember me."

AGNUS DEI

¶ *The Choir may sing*

Agnus Dei, qui tollis peccata mundi, miserere nobis.

Agnus Dei, qui tollis peccata mundi, miserere nobis.

Agnus Dei, qui tollis peccata mundi, done nobis pacem.

Lamb of God, you take away the sins of the world, have mercy on us.

Lamb of God, you take away the sins of the world, have mercy on us.

Lamb of God, you take away the sins of the world, grant us peace.

We break this bread to share in the brokenness of Christ

Though we are many, we are one body, for we all share in the one bread.

INVITATION TO COMMUNION

Jesus is the bread of life, and is present to us in this meal. So eat this bread, and drink this wine. In these actions, God welcomes us, so that we might welcome him.

¶ *The choir receives communion first, followed by the congregation. Everyone is welcome to receive communion. If you do not wish to receive communion, then you are welcome to come forward to receive a blessing, in which case please cross your arms at your chest.*

MOTET (An anthem sung by the Choir)

PRAYER AFTER COMMUNION

God of every epoch, and every Galaxy.
God of every split second and every square inch.
God of truth and justice.
You are with us, our peace, our security, our hope.
You who removes the barriers that divide us, and transgresses that boundaries separate us, make us one with each other, and one with you. To the glory of your name.

¶ *All Stand*

HYMN

¶ *Remain Standing*

May God-in-relationship, enrich your relationships:
May the God of power, enable you to flourish.
May the God of vulnerability, show you true strength.
May the Spirit of his presence, embrace you, enfold you, encourage you.
Now and always.
Amen.

8

A Second Order for Choral Communion

¶ *All stand*

OPENING SENTENCE

HYMN

¶ *Please remain standing, if you are able*

Almighty and everlasting God.
   We praise you as the God who meets with us,
   In all our frailty and failure.
   Who rejoices with us,
   In all our thankfulness and joy
   Who celebrates with us,
   In all our triumphs and gains.

So awaken us more fully to who we are,
   Who we are to others and to you.
   In your presence,

May our delusion meet reality.
May our pretension meet truth.
May our despair meet hope.
In your presence, we are reminded that
We have failed others, and in so doing, failed you.
We have turned a blind eye to those who needed our help.
We have thought and spoken wrongly of others.
We have chosen not to hear uncomfortable truth about the
world, and about our place in it.

Leave us not in debt to one another.
Restore our relationships with others.
Deepen our trust in them and in you.
For the sake of your name.
Amen.

¶ *The choir may sing*
  Kyrie eleison,
  Christe eleison
  Kyrie eleison.

Lord have mercy,
  Christ have mercy,
  Lord, have mercy.

¶ *All sit*

THE FIRST READING

At the end
  Thanks be to God

¶ *All stand*

Loving God, we worship you as the Lord of space and time, who meets us here and now.

You are the God of creation
Who brings something out of nothing.
You are the God of salvation
Who brings hope out of failure.
You are the God of liberation
Who brings justice for those who have been denied it.
You are the Lord of Hosts
Who was born into an occupied territory.
You are the Lord of eternity,
Who became a peasant tradesman.
You are the Lord Almighty,
At home in the lowest echelons of society.
You are the Lord of heaven and earth,
Who became marginalised, outcast, excluded.
You are the Lord God,
whose power is expressed in powerlessness.

¶ *Remain standing*

HYMN

¶ *Remain standing*

THE HOLY GOSPEL
   At the end,
   Thanks be to God.

¶ *All sit*

THE ADDRESS

INTERCESSIONS

Ending with
> **Loving God in heaven, hallowed be your name,**
> **Your kingdom come,**
> **Your will be done on earth as in heaven.**
> **Give us today our daily bread.**
> **Forgive us our sins as we forgive those who sin against us.**
> **Lead us not into temptation but deliver us from evil,**
> **For the kingdom, the power and the glory are yours,**
> **Now and evermore. Amen.**

¶ *All stand*

THE GREAT THANKSGIVING

The Lord be with you.
> **And with your spirit.**
Lift up your hearts.
> **We lift them to the Lord.**
Let us give thanks to the Lord our God.
> **It is right and just.**

It is right and just to offer you our thanks, because you are the Creator God, vast beyond our understanding, holy beyond our comprehension, beautiful beyond our perception. And yet you are the source of all life, creator of every hair on our head, maker of every atom in our body. Wholly unapproachable, unreachable, and yet, you reach out to us. And so we respond, with the voice of the church through the ages,

Sanctus, Sanctus, Sanctus,
  Dominus Deus Sabaoth
  Pleni sunt coeli et terra gloria tua.
  Hosanna in excelsis.

Or

Holy, holy, holy,
  Lord God of hosts,
  Heaven and earth are full of Thy glory.
  Hosanna in the highest.

You are indeed Holy, Other, Separate and Distant, but you come to us in the person of Jesus and by the presence of your Holy Spirit, you draw all creatures to you. And so, by your grace, we may grow in grace, in holiness, in Christ-likeness, so that we may offer you the praise worthy of your name.

Make this meal holy then, by the power of your Spirit, so that this food and this drink may be to us the body and blood of your Son, Jesus Christ.

Not long before his arrest, Jesus took some bread in his rough, tradesman's hands, and raised his eyes to heaven. He gave you thanks, said a blessing, broke the bread, and handed it to his followers, saying: "All of you should eat this, because this is my body which will be given up for you."

In the same way, after supper, he took a cup of wine and, in the rough skin of his hands, he gave you thanks, said a blessing, and gave the cup to his followers, saying: "All of you should drink this, because this is the cup of my own blood. The blood of the new covenant, which is bled for you and for many, for the cancellation of debt. You should do this to remember me."

Lord Jesus,
As we eat this bread and drink this wine, we proclaim your death, until you come again.
And so, as we celebrate the death and resurrection, we hold before you, the body and blood of your dear Son, and thank you for drawing us into your holy presence.

We pray that as we share in the body and blood of Christ, we may be gathered as one, by the power of your holy Spirit.

We praise you, with all who stand before you in earth and heaven, Lord Almighty, throughout all ages, world without end. **Amen**

¶ *All sit*

THE BREAKING OF THE BREAD

We break this bread to share in the body of Christ
Though we are many, we are one body, for we all share in the one bread

AGNUS DEI

¶ *The Choir may sing*
Agnus Dei, qui tollis peccata mundi, miserere nobis.
Agnus Dei, qui tollis peccata mundi, miserere nobis.
Agnus Dei, qui tollis peccata mundi, done nobis pacem.

Lamb of God, you take away the sins of the world, have mercy on us.

Lamb of God, you take away the sins of the world, have mercy on us.

Lamb of God, you take away the sins of the world, grant us peace.

INVITATION TO COMMUNION

In this meal, Jesus has promised to make himself present.

In this bread, we share his brokenness, as he shares ours.

In this wine, we remember his sacrifice, and offer him our sacrifice of praise.

¶ *The choir receives communion first, followed by the congregation. Everyone is welcome to receive communion. If you do not wish to receive communion, then you are welcome to come forward to receive a blessing, in which case please cross your arms at your chest.*

MOTET (An anthem sung by the choir)

PRAYER AFTER COMMUNION

O God of truth and justice, we hold before you those whose memory we cherish, and those whose names we will never know. Help us to lift our eyes above the torment of this broken world, and grant us the grace to pray for those who wish us harm. As we honour the past, may we put our faith in your future; for you are the source of life and hope, now and for ever. **Amen.**

¶ *All Stand*

HYMN

¶ *Remain Standing*

God who provides,
We thank you for this meal.
God of the hungry,
Help us share our wealth with others.
God of brokenness,
May we face the pain in ourselves, and the pain of the world.

God of wholeness,
Make us whole,
God of grace,
Make us gracious.
God of peace,
Make us channels of your peace.
Amen

9

A Third Order for Choral Communion

We meet in the name of Immanuel, Mother and Father of all peoples, Creator of all life and of each life,

God with us.

We meet in the name of Immanuel, liberator of all who are oppressed, welcomer of all who are excluded,

God with us.

We meet in the name of Immanuel, breaking down old mindsets, inviting us into new worldviews,

God with us.

Lord Immanuel,

Meet with us here,
Liberate us here,
Remake us here.

HYMN (see board for hymn numbers)

BIBLE READING

HYMN

THE STORY

Jesus, a powerless young man who had disappointed the crowds, had nevertheless wrought havoc in the Holy City, and became a matter of concern to authorities keen to maintain order. He knew his end was nearing, when he and his followers gathered to eat in a dim lit upstairs room in that city. He knew the danger well enough. He knew that later that night, one of them would hand him over to the authorities. In all likelihood, he knew they would torture and execute him.

Even so, he hosted a meal. He took a chunk of bread and broke it. "This is my body," he said. "Broken. For you. Do this to reunite with me."

Later, once they had eaten, he took a cup of wine. "This is the new relationship with God," he said. "It is made possible because of my death. Drink this, all of you, to reunite with me."

Today, from the safety offered by distance and time, we seek to follow his command. We share this bread and this wine. This food and drink represents creation's gift, and humanity's labours. At this meal, Jesus communicates his presence. At this meal, we may reunite with him.

¶ *The choir may sing*
Kyrie eleison,
Christe eleison
Kyrie eleison.

HYMN

THE EUCHARIST PRAYER

Lord of all eternity
Be present with us now.
Every fibre of our being,
Is drawn towards you.
You deserve our gratitude and praise,
And we give them gladly.

It is with gladness that we praise and thank you, because you have created everything that has brought us into being, and brought us right into this time and place. All that brings life, and all that brings joy, bears the hallmark of your handiwork. All that brings love, and all that inspires love, beats with your divine pulse.

And so, we praise you for the world in which we live, and move, and have our being; for the universe beyond our knowledge and sight; for the wonders of the everyday that so often we miss.

From within this world's sorrow and its joy, its injustice and its complexity, you greet us in the person of Jesus. For his humility and his audacity, for his brutal honesty and aggressive compassion, for his unwavering resolve and his spontaneous grace, we praise you.

We praise you, whom we encounter here and now in the person of the Holy Spirit, who draws us closer to one another, and – in so doing – to you. And so, by your spirit, we readily join our voices to the song of the church that echoes through the ages,

Holy, Other, Wholly Other,
  God of strength and power,
  Your being floods light through heaven and earth.
  All brilliance is yours, the highest power.
  Make this true.

True hope is voiced, from the depths of despair,
  Hope in the coming of God's own envoy.
  So come,
  Free us now,
  By heaven's decree.

¶ *The Choir may sing:*
  Sanctus, Sanctus, Sanctus,
  Dominus Deus Sabaoth
  Pleni sunt coeli et terra gloria tua.
  Hosanna in excelsis.

And, since you have given more than your words alone, and ask us for more than words alone can express, we silence ourselves in your life-changing presence.

Word-become-flesh, may your living Word be made flesh in our lives:

Displace our knowledge with your questions.

Question our certainties with your disturbance.

Disturb our comfort with the living presence of him whose food we now share.

Silence is kept

God of loving-kindness, fill us with your Holy Spirit as we share this meal. May this bread and this wine become, for us, the body and blood of Jesus. And, by your grace, alert us to your presence, awaken us to your Spirit, remake us in your image.

THE BREAKING OF BREAD

Jesus was with his friends, gathered at the table, when he took bread, broke it, and said, "This is my body – broken for you."

Later, he held up a cup of wine and said, "This is the new relationship with God, enabled by my death. Take it, each of you, to reunite with me."

Jesus, the baby laid in a feeding trough.
Meet us in our weakness
Jesus, outcast and outsider, rejected and excluded,
Embrace us as we are.
Jesus, whose power is known only through weakness,
Grant us your peace.
Jesus, liberator of all,
Make us channels of your grace.

Creator of the galaxies, you meet us as we eat this bread.
Liberator of the oppressed, you meet us in this cup.
And so, we eat this bread and drink this wine. In them, God unites with us, and we with him.

¶ *The Choir may sing*
Agnus Dei, qui tollis peccata mundi, miserere nobis.
Agnus Dei, qui tollis peccata mundi, miserere nobis.
Agnus Dei, qui tollis peccata mundi, done nobis pacem.

All are welcome to receive communion. The Choir comes forward to receive communion. Once seated, they are followed by the congregation.

Jesus of Nazareth is the source of our peace. Allies and enemies, strangers and friends, folk of any age and any gender, of any nation and any class, he has overcome all that might keep us apart, and rooted our beings in him and in one another.

HYMN (or a Motet sung by the choir)

ADDRESS

PRAYER

HYMN

CONCLUDING PRAYER
   May Christ's life be ever in our minds,
   And our lives modelled on his.
   May the fears he faced, be felt in our guts
   And our fears shaped by his.
   May the courage he showed, be at work in our hearts
   And our hearts inspired by his.
   May the grace he shared, be rooted in our spirits,
   And his grace made known through our lives.

10

Holy Communion for All Saints

¶ *All stand*

OPENING SENTENCE

HYMN (see boards for hymn numbers)

¶ *All sit*

Almighty God, who sees as we are, and loves us as we are, fill us afresh with your Holy Spirit, that the lives of those who have gone before us in the faith may echo through our walk with you in the present, through Jesus Christ our Lord.**Amen.**

Let us confess our sins to God.
   Most merciful God,
   Father of our Lord Jesus Christ,
   We confess that to you and in the company of all God's people,

We have wronged you and wronged others,
In what we have said and not said,
In what we have done and not done.
In your loving kindness,
Clear us of all debt,
Credit us with justice,
And make us channels of your grace;
That our action may be fair,
And our love for others may reflect your love for us.
Amen.

¶ *The choir may sing*
Kyrie eleison,
Christe eleison
Kyrie eleison.

Lord have mercy,
Christ have mercy,
Lord have mercy

If we confess our failures, God is loyal and fair, and will clear our debts, and guide us from all injustice.
Amen. Thanks be to God.

¶ *All sit*

THE FIRST READING
At the end
Hear the Word of the Lord.
Thanks be to God

¶ *All stand*

Glory to God in the highest,
   And peace to his people on earth.
   Lord God, heavenly King, almighty God and Father,
   We worship you, we give you thanks, we praise you for your glory.
   Lord Jesus Christ, Only Begotten Son,
   Lord God, Lamb of God, Son of the Father,
   You take away the sin of the world:
   Have mercy on us.
   You are seated at the right hand of the Father:
   Receive our prayer.
   For you alone are the Holy One,
   You alone are the Lord,
   You alone are the Most High,
   Jesus Christ, with the Holy Spirit, in the glory of God the Father.

¶ *Remain standing*

HYMN

¶ *Remain standing*

Almighty God,
   As the body of Christ, we take our place in the corner of time and space you have granted to us.
   May we learn from the best of your followers in the past,
   So that by your grace we might become an inspiration for those in the future.

And so, may we your body, become a means by which your love touches the world here and now.

By the power of the Holy Spirit, may those with whom our own lives interweave, encounter your grace in our lives.

To the glory of your name. **Amen.**

THE HOLY GOSPEL
At the end
Hear the word of the Lord
Thanks be to God

¶ *All sit*

THE ADDRESS

PRAYERS OF INTERCESSION
Ending with
With your followers through all ages, let us address their God and ours with the words that Jesus gave:
Our Father, who art in heaven,
hallowed be thy name;
thy kingdom come,
thy will be done
on earth as it is in heaven.
Give us this day our daily bread,
and forgive us our trespasses,
as we forgive those who trespass against us;
and lead us not into temptation,
but deliver us from evil.

THE GREAT THANKSGIVING

¶ *All stand*

We give you thanks, for the hope we share with those who have gone before us in their walk with you. Seeing their commitment, hearing their voice, learning from their example, may we today truly be the body of Christ on earth, as the Word is made flesh in our life together. And so we join our voices with all who have gone before us, and all who will come after us, for ever praising you and singing / saying

Sanctus, Sanctus, Sanctus,
  Dominus Deus Sabaoth
  Pleni sunt coeli et terra gloria tua.
  Hosanna in excelsis.

Holy, holy, holy,
  Lord God of Sabaoth
  heaven and earth are full of Thy glory.
  Hosanna in the highest.

And so, calling to our minds, and feeling in our guts, the terrible threat and the profound assurance of your holiness, your radical difference, your sheer otherness, we ask that – by the power of your Holy Spirit – this bread and this wine may be for us, the broken body and the spilled blood, of Jesus Christ our Liberator, who, on the same night he was handed over to the authorities, took a piece of bread, gave you thanks, and broke it to share with his followers, saying:

  "Take and eat this. It is my body which is given for you. You should do this to remember me."

In the same way, after the meal he took the cup, gave you thanks, and gave it to them, saying, "Drink this, each one of you. It is my blood of the New Testament, which is bled for you and for many for the clearing of debts. You should do this every time you drink it, to remember me."

Praise to you, Lord Jesus:

Dying you destroyed our death,
rising you restored our life:
Lord Jesus, come in glory.

And so, loving God, remembering his execution at the hands of the best the world had to offer, the sacrifice made for the sins of the world; rejoicing in his resurrection and ascension, and looking for his future presence, we celebrate this meal as a sign of our liberation. As we bring our sacrifice of praise, we offer this bread and this cup, and we thank you for inviting us into your presence. May your Holy Spirit be among us and all people who share this one bread and one up, so that we – in the company of all your people throughout space and time, may praise and glorify you as you deserve, through Jesus Christ our Lord; by whom, and with whom and in whom, in the unity of the Holy Spirit, we worship you, almighty and Loving God, throughout all ages, world without end.

Amen

¶ *All sit*

THE BREAKING OF THE BREAD

We break this bread to share in the body of Christ

Though we are many, we are one body, for we all share in the one bread.

AGNUS DEI

¶ The Choir may sing

Agnus Dei, qui tollis peccata mundi, miserere nobis.

Agnus Dei, qui tollis peccata mundi, miserere nobis.

Agnus Dei, qui tollis peccata mundi, done nobis pacem.

Lamb of God, you take away the sins of the world, have mercy on us.

Lamb of God, you take away the sins of the world, have mercy on us.

Lamb of God, you take away the sins of the world, grant us peace.

INVITATION TO COMMUNION

Jesus is the living bread which came down from heaven:

If anyone eats of this bread, they will live forever.

Lord, give us this bread always.

¶ The choir receives communion first, followed by the congregation. Everyone is welcome to receive communion. If you do not wish to receive communion, then you are welcome to come forward to receive a blessing, in which case please cross your arms at your chest.

MOTET (An anthem sung by the Choir)

PRAYER AFTER COMMUNION

O God of truth and justice, we hold before you those whose memory we cherish, and those whose names we will never know. Help us to lift our eyes above the torment of this broken world, and grant us the grace to pray for those with whom we disagree, those who wish us harm, and those whose presence challenges all that is dear to us.

As we honour the past, may we put our faith in your future; for you are the source of life and hope, now and for ever. **Amen.**

¶ *All Stand*

HYMN

¶ *Remain Standing*

The blessing of God, the Father the Son and the Holy Spirit, remain with us always.

Amen.

Go in peace in the power of the Spirit to live and work to God's praise and glory.

Thanks be to God. Amen.

11

An Order for Congregational Communion

We meet in the name of Immanuel, Mother and Father of all peoples, Creator of all life and of each life,

God with us.

We meet in the name of Immanuel, liberator of all who are oppressed, welcomer of all who are excluded,

God with us.

We meet in the name of Immanuel, breaking down old mindsets, inviting us into new worldviews,

God with us.

Lord Immanuel,

Meet with us here,

Liberate us here,

Remake us here.

HYMN (see board for hymn numbers)

BIBLE READING

HYMN / ANTHEM

THE STORY

Jesus, a powerless young man who had disappointed the crowds, had nevertheless wrought havoc in the Holy City, and became a matter of concern to authorities keen to maintain order. He knew his end was nearing, when he and his followers gathered to eat in a dim lit upstairs room in that city. He knew the danger well enough. He knew that later that night, one of them would hand him over to the authorities. In all likelihood, he knew they would torture and execute him.

Even so, he hosted a meal. He took a chunk of bread and broke it. "This is my body," he said. "Broken. For you. Do this to reunite with me."

Later, once they had eaten, he took a cup of wine. "This is the new relationship with God," he said. "It is made possible because of my death. Drink this, all of you, to reunite with me."

Today, from the safety granted by distance and time, we seek to follow his command. We share this bread and this wine. This food and drink represents creation's gift, and humanity's labours. At this meal, Jesus communicates his presence. At this meal, we may reunite with him.

THE EUCHARIST PRAYER

Lord of all eternity
Be present with us now.
Every fibre of our being,
Is drawn towards you.

You deserve our gratitude and praise,
And we give them gladly.

It is with gladness that we praise and thank you, because you have created everything that has brought us into being, and brought us right into this time and place. All that brings life, and all that brings joy, bears the hallmark of your handiwork. All that brings love, and all that inspires love, beats with your divine pulse.

And so, we praise you for the world in which we live, and move, and have our being; for the universe beyond our knowledge and sight; for the wonders of the everyday that so often we miss.

From within this world's sorrow and its joy, its injustice and its complexity, you greet us in the person of Jesus. For his humility and his audacity, for his brutal honesty and aggressive compassion, for his unwavering resolve and his spontaneous grace, we praise you.

We praise you, whom we encounter here and now in the person of the Holy Spirit, who draws us closer to one another, and – in so doing – to you. And so, by your Spirit, we readily join our voices to the song of the church that echoes through the ages,

Holy, Other,
Wholly Other,
God of strength and power,
Your being floods light through heaven and earth.
All brilliance is yours, the highest power.
Make this true.

For true hope is voiced
  From the depths of despair.
  Hope in the coming of God's own envoy.
  So come,
  Free us now,
  By heaven's decree.

And, since you have given more than your words alone, and ask us for more than words alone can express, we silence ourselves in your life-changing presence.

Word-become-flesh, may your living Word be made flesh in our lives:

Displace our knowledge with your questions.

Question our certainties with your disturbance.

Disturb our comfort with the living presence of him whose food we now share.

Silence is kept

God of loving-kindness, fill us with your Holy Spirit as we share this meal. May this bread and this wine become, for us, the body and blood of Jesus. And, by your grace, alert us to your presence, awaken us to your Spirit, remake us in your image.

THE BREAKING OF BREAD

Jesus was with his friends, gathered at the table, when he took bread, broke it, and said, "This is my body – broken for you."

Later, he held up a cup of wine and said, "This is the new relationship with God, enabled by my death. Take it, each of you, to reunite with me."

Jesus, the baby laid in a feeding trough.
Meet us in our weakness
Jesus, outcast and outsider, rejected and excluded,
Embrace us as we are.
Jesus, whose power is known only through weakness,
Grant us your peace.
Jesus, liberator of all,
Make us channels of your grace.

Creator of the galaxies, you meet us as we eat this bread.
Liberator of the oppressed, you meet us in this cup.
And so, we eat this bread and drink this wine. In them, God unites with us, and we with him.

All are welcome to receive communion. The Choir comes forward to receive communion. Once seated, they are followed by the congregation.

Jesus of Nazareth is the source of our peace. Allies and enemies, strangers and friends, folk of any age and any gender, of any nation and any class, he has overcome all that might keep us apart, and rooted our beings in him and in one another.

HYMN

ADDRESS

PRAYER

HYMN

CONCLUDING PRAYER

May Christ's life be ever in our minds,
And our lives modelled on his.
May the fears he faced, be felt in our guts,
And our fears shaped by his.
May the courage he showed, be at work in our hearts,
And our hearts inspired by his.
May the grace he shared, be rooted in our spirits,
And his grace made known through in our lives,
Amen.

III

TRADITIONAL SERVICES

12

Compline

¶ Please stand if you are able as the Choir and Clergy enter.

PREPARATION
The Lord Almighty grant us a quiet night and a perfect end.
Amen.
Our help is in the name of the Lord
who hath made heaven and earth.

A period of silence is held for reflection on the past day.

¶ Please be seated.

Let us humbly confess our sins unto Almighty God.
Most merciful God,
we confess to you,
before the whole company of heaven and one another,
that we have sinned in thought, word and deed
and in what we have failed to do.
Forgive us our sins,

heal us by your Spirit,
and raise us to new life in Christ.
Amen.

Cantor O God, make speed to save us.
  Choir O Lord, make haste to help us.
  Cantor Glory be to the Father, and to the Son: and to the Holy Ghost.
  Choir As it was in the beginning, is now and ever shall be, world without end. Amen.
  Cantor Praise ye the Lord.
  Choir The Lord's name be praised.

The Choir sing the Office Hymn Te lucis ante terminum *to the Ferial melody.*

Cantor Before the ending of the day
  Choir Creator of the world we pray,
  That with thy wonted favour thou
  Wouldst be our guard and keeper now.
  From all ill dreams defend our eyes,
  from nightly fears and fantasies;
  tread under foot our ghostly foe,
  that no pollution we may know.
  O Father that we ask be done,
  through Jesus Christ thine only Son,
  who with the Holy Ghost and thee,
  doth live and reign eternally. Amen.

THE WORD OF GOD
  The Choir sing the Antiphon *and* Psalm 134.

Cantor Have mercy upon me, O God, and hearken unto my prayer.

Choir Behold, now, praise the Lord: all ye servants of the Lord;

Ye that by night stand in the house of the Lord:

even in the courts of the house of our God.

Lift up your heads in the sanctuary: and praise the Lord.

The Lord that made heaven and earth:

give thee blessing out of Sion.

Glory be to the Father, and to the Son, and to the Holy Ghost.

As it was in the beginning, is now, and ever shall be:

world without end.

Amen.

Cantor Have mercy upon me, O God, and hearken unto my prayer.

The Priest reads a passage of Scripture *from Revelation* 22.

The servants of the Lamb shall see the face of God, whose name will be on their foreheads. There will be no more night: they will not need the light of a lamp or the light of the sun, for God will be their light, and they will reign for ever and ever.

Thanks be to God.

The Choir sing the Responsory, Antiphon, *and* Gospel Canticle.

Cantor Into thy hands, O Lord, I commend my spirit.

Choir Into thy hands, O Lord, I commend my spirit.

Cantor For thou hast redeemed me, O Lord, thou God of truth.

Choir I commend my spirit.

Cantor Glory be to the Father, and to the Son, and to the Holy

Ghost.

Choir I commend my spirit.

Cantor Keep me as the apple of an eye.

Choir Hide me under the shadow of thy wings.

Choir Preserve us, O Lord, while waking,

and guard us while sleeping,

that awake we may watch with Christ,

and asleep we may rest in peace.

Lord, now lettest thou thy servant depart in peace

according to thy word.

For mine eyes have seen thy salvation,

Which thou hast prepared before the face of all people;

To be a light to lighten the Gentiles,

and to be the glory of thy people Israel.

Glory be to the Father, and to the Son, and to the Holy Ghost.

As it was in the beginning, is now, and ever shall be:

world without end. Amen.

The Choir repeat the Antiphon.

PRAYERS

Cantor Lord, have mercy upon us.

Choir Christ, have mercy upon us.

Cantor Lord, have mercy upon us.

The Choir sing a choral setting of The Lord's Prayer.

Cantor Blessed art thou, Lord God of our fathers:

Choir to be praised and glorified above all for ever.

Cantor Let us bless the Father, the Son, and the Holy Ghost:

Choir let us praise and magnify him forever.

Cantor Blessed art thou, O Lord, in the firmament of heaven:

Choir to be praised and glorified above all for ever.
Cantor The almighty and most merciful Lord,
guard us and give us his blessing.
Choir Amen.
Choir Visit this place, O Lord, we pray,
and drive far from it the snares of the enemy;
may your holy angels dwell with us and guard us in peace,
and may your blessing be always upon us;
through Jesus Christ our Lord. Amen.
Look down, O God, from your heavenly throne,
illuminate the darkness of this night with your celestial
brightness,
and from the children of light banish the deeds of darkness;
through Jesus Christ our Saviour. Amen.
Watch, O Lord, with those who wake, or watch, or weep
tonight, and give
Your angels and saints charge over those who sleep.
Tend Your sick ones, O Lord Christ.
Rest Your weary ones, Bless Your dying ones.
Soothe Your suffering ones, Pity Your afflicted ones.
Shield Your joyous ones, and all for Your love's sake. Amen.

The Choir sing an Anthem, *followed by a period of silence for
private prayer.*

THE CONCLUSION

Cantor We will lay us down in peace and take our rest.
Choir For it is thou, Lord, only that makes us dwell in safety.
Cantor Abide with us, O Lord,
Choir for it is toward evening and the day is far spent.

Cantor As the watchmen look for the morning,

Choir so do we look for thee, O Christ.

Cantor The Lord be with you.

Choir And with thy spirit.

Cantor Let us bless the Lord.

Choir Thanks be to God.

Cantor The almighty and merciful Lord, the Father, the Son, and the Holy Ghost, bless us and preserve us.

Choir Amen.

¶ *Please stand if you are able as the Choir and Clergy depart in silence.*

13

Choral Evensong

¶ *Please stand if you are able as the Choir and Clergy enter.*

On Feast Days, an INTROIT *may be sung.*

PRECES
   Cantor O Lord, open thou our lips.
   Choir And our mouth shall show forth thy praise.
   Cantor O God, make speed to save us.
   Choir O Lord, make haste to help us.
   Cantor Glory be to the Father, and to the Son, and to the Holy Ghost;
   Choir As it was in the beginning, is now, and ever shall be, world without end. Amen.
   Cantor Praise ye the Lord.
   Choir The Lord's Name be praised.

¶ *Please be seated as the Choir sings the psalm(s) for the day.*

PSALMODY

FIRST READING
¶ *Please remain seated*

MAGNIFICAT

My soul doth magnify the Lord: and my spirit hath rejoiced in God my Saviour.

For he hath regarded: the lowliness of his handmaiden.

For behold, from henceforth: all generations shall call me blessed.

For he that is mighty hath magnified me: and holy is his Name.

And his mercy is on them that fear him: throughout all generations.

He hath showed strength with his arm:

he hath scattered the proud in the imagination of their hearts.

He hath put down the mighty from their seat: and hath exalted the humble and meek.

He hath filled the hungry with good things: and the rich he hath sent empty away.

He remembering his mercy hath holpen his servant Israel: as he promised to our forefathers, Abraham and his seed, for ever.

Glory be to the Father, and to the Son, and to the Holy Ghost;

As it was in the beginning, is now, and ever shall be, world without end. Amen.

SECOND READING

NUNC DIMITTIS

Lord, now lettest thou thy servant depart in peace: according to thy word.

For mine eyes have seen: thy salvation,

Which thou hast prepared: before the face of all people;

To be a light to lighten the Gentiles: and to be the glory of thy people Israel.

Glory be to the Father, and to the Son, and to the Holy Ghost;

As it was in the beginning, is now, and ever shall be, world without end. Amen.

¶ *Please stand if you are able as we say together:*

APOSTLES' CREED

I believe in God the Father almighty,
maker of heaven and earth:
and in Jesus Christ his only Son our Lord,
who was conceived by the Holy Ghost,
born of the Virgin Mary,
suffered under Pontius Pilate,
was crucified, dead, and buried.
He descended into hell;
the third day he rose again from the dead;
he ascended into heaven,
and sitteth on the right hand of God the Father almighty;
from thence he shall come to judge the quick and the dead.
I believe in the Holy Ghost;

the holy catholick Church;
the communion of saints;
the forgiveness of sins;
the resurrection of the body,
and the life everlasting. Amen.

RESPONSES

Cantor The Lord be with you.

Choir And with thy spirit.

Cantor Let us pray.

¶ *Please be seated.*

Choir Lord, have mercy upon us. Christ, have mercy upon us. Lord, have mercy upon us.

Our Father, which art in heaven, Hallowed be thy Name. Thy kingdom come. Thy will be done in earth, As it is in heaven. Give us this day our daily bread. And forgive us our trespasses, As we forgive them that trespass against us. And lead us not into temptation, But deliver us from evil. Amen.

Cantor O Lord, shew thy mercy upon us.

Choir And grant us thy salvation.

Cantor O Lord, save the Queen.

Choir And mercifully hear us when we call upon thee.

Cantor Endue thy Ministers with righteousness.

Choir And make thy chosen people joyful.

Cantor O Lord, save thy people.

Choir And bless thine inheritance.

Cantor Give peace in our time, O Lord.

Choir Because there is none other that fighteth for us, but only thou, O God.

Cantor O God, make clean our hearts within us.

Choir And take not thy Holy Spirit from us.

COLLECTS

The Collect of the day is sung, followed by:

O God, from whom all holy desires, all good counsels, and all just works do proceed; give unto thy servants that peace which the world cannot give; that both, our hearts may be set to obey thy commandments, and also that, by thee, we being defended from the fear of our enemies may pass our time in rest and quietness; through the merits of Jesus Christ our Saviour. *Amen.*

Lighten our darkness, we beseech thee, O Lord; and by thy great mercy defend us from all perils and dangers of this night; for the love of thy only Son, our Saviour, Jesus Christ. *Amen.*

CHOIR ANTHEM

PRAYERS

Ending with,

Almighty God, who hast given us grace at this time with one accord to make our common supplications unto thee; and dost promise that when two or three are gathered together in thy Name thou wilt grant their requests: Fulfil now, O Lord, the desires and petitions of thy servants, as may be most expedient for them; granting us in this world knowledge of thy truth, and in the world to come life everlasting. **Amen.**

¶ *Please be seatedPlease stand if you are able as we say together:*

The grace of our Lord Jesus Christ,
    and the love of God
    and the fellowship of the Holy Spirit
    be with us all evermore.
    Amen.

VOLUNTARY

14

Communion

¶ *All stand*

OPENING SENTENCE

HYMN

¶ *All sit*

Almighty God, to whom all hearts are open, all desires known, and from whom no secrets are hidden: cleans the thoughts of our hearts, by the inspiration of your Holy Spirit, that we may perfectly love you, and worthily magnify your holy Name; through Christ our Lord.
   Amen.

Let us confess our sins to God.

Most merciful God,
Father of our Lord Jesus Christ,
we confess that we have sinned
in thought, word and deed.
We have not loved you with our whole heart.
We have not loved our neighbours as ourselves.
In your mercy
forgive what we have been,
help us to amend what we are,
and direct what we shall be;
that we may do justly,
love mercy,
and walk humbly with you, our God.
Amen.

¶ *The choir may sing*

Kyrie eleison,
Christe eleison
Kyrie eleison.

Lord have mercy,
Christ have mercy,
Lord have mercy

If we confess our sins, God is faithful and just, and will forgive us our sins, and cleanse us from all unrighteousness.
Amen. Thanks be to God.

¶ *All sit*

THE FIRST READING
At the end
Hear the word of the Lord
Thanks be to God

¶ *All stand*

Glory to God in the highest,
And peace to his people on earth.
Lord God, heavenly King, almighty God and Father,
We worship you, we give you thanks, we praise you for your glory.
Lord Jesus Christ, Only Begotten Son,
Lord God, Lamb of God, Son of the Father,
You take away the sin of the world:
Have mercy on us.
You are seated at the right hand of the Father:
Receive our prayer.
For you alone are the Holy One,
You alone are the Lord,
You alone are the Most High,
Jesus Christ, with the Holy Spirit, in the glory of God the Father.

¶ *Remain standing*

HYMN

¶ *Remain standing*

THE HOLY GOSPEL
At the end
Hear the word of the Lord
Thanks be to God

¶ *All sit*

THE ADDRESS

PRAYERS OF INTERCESSION
Ending with
Our Father, who art in heaven,
hallowed be thy name;
thy kingdom come,
thy will be done
on earth as it is in heaven.
Give us this day our daily bread,
and forgive us our trespasses,
as we forgive those who trespass against us;
and lead us not into temptation,
but deliver us from evil.

THE GREAT THANKSGIVING

¶ *All stand*

The Lord be with you:
And also with you

Lift up your hearts:
We lift them to the Lord
Let us give thanks to the Lord our God:
It is right to give thanks and praise

¶ *The celebrant continues with the prayer, ending with...*
   "...for ever praising you and singing..."

Sanctus, Sanctus, Sanctus,
   Dominus Deus Sabaoth
   Pleni sunt coeli et terra gloria tua.
   Hosanna in excelsis.

Holy, holy, holy,
   Lord God of Sabaoth
   heaven and earth are full of Thy glory.
   Hosanna in the highest.
      ¶ *During the Eucharistic prayer the celebrant says:*

...Praise to you, Lord Jesus:
   All **Dying you destroyed our death,**
    rising you restored our life:
    Lord Jesus, come in glory.

At the end of the Eucharistic prayer
   ...with all who stand before you in earth and heaven,
   we worship you, Father almighty, throughout all ages world
without end.
   All **Amen**

¶ *All sit*

THE BREAKING OF THE BREAD

We break this bread to share in the body of Christ
Though we are many, we are one body, for we all share in the one bread

AGNUS DEI

¶ *The Choir may sing*
Agnus Dei, qui tollis peccata mundi, miserere nobis.
Agnus Dei, qui tollis peccata mundi, miserere nobis.
Agnus Dei, qui tollis peccata mundi, done nobis pacem.

Lamb of God, you take away the sins of the world, have mercy on us.
Lamb of God, you take away the sins of the world, have mercy on us.
Lamb of God, you take away the sins of the world, grant us peace.

INVITATION TO COMMUNION

Jesus is the living bread which came down from heaven:
If anyone eats of this bread, they will live forever.
Lord, give us this bread always.

¶ *The choir receives communion first, followed by the congregation. Everyone is welcome to receive communion. If you do not wish to receive communion, then you are welcome to come forward to receive a blessing, in which case please cross your arms at your chest.*

MOTET (An anthem sung by the Choir)

PRAYER AFTER COMMUNION

We thank you, Almighty and ever loving God, because you do not exclude us, but invite us to your table and share your gifts with us. By the power of your Holy Spirit, may we reflect the generosity of your Son, and by your grace, may we - here and now - be your gift to others. To the glory of your name. **Amen.**

¶ *All Stand*

HYMN

¶ *Remain Standing*

The blessing of God, the Father the Son and the Holy Spirit, remain with us always.
Amen.
Go in peace in the power of the Spirit to live and work to God's praise and glory.
Thanks be to God. Amen.

IV

PRAYERS OF INTERCESSION

15

Intercessions for Lent Term (Jan - Apr)

NEW YEAR

As we enter this new year, we bring before you our hopes and dreams, our aims and objectives, the best of our intentions and the worthiest of our ambitions.

We bring before you all that we hope to make out of this year, and submit it all to your life-changing grace.

When our priorities submerge us in pointless tasks,

When our ambitions fail us or overtake us,

When our hopes seek the fulfilment of none but ourselves,

When our hearts deceive us to think that we are right when we are not

Open our eyes to who you really are.

Open our eyes that we might see the future you have already planned for us.

Grant us:

the courage to seek your kingdom;

the energy to labour where labour is needed;
the wisdom to see when it is not;
the grace to be quiet when we need to listen,
the humility to receive from others,
the compassion to hear and see and love those who nobody wants to hear and see and love.

By your loving-kindness, make us the body of Christ, thriving by the indwelling of your Spirit, bringing glory to God the Father.

HOMELESSNESS SUNDAY

Loving Father, we pray today for rough sleepers and homeless people, and about the causes of homelessness. We pray for those who live in abusive homes, those who suffer relationship breakdowns, those who become addicted to drugs and alcohol. Where there is abuse we pray for justice, where there is sorrow we pray for comfort, where there is addiction we pray for freedom.

Son of man, with nowhere to lay your head, we pray for the hundreds in our cities who will sleep rough tonight. May the organisations working with such people be well supported and equipped. May they truly be channels of your grace, that they may lead people into the wholeness for which they were created.

Holy Spirit, kindle in us a compassion that leads to action. Free us from comfort, indifference and fear, that we might embrace those who are forgotten, broken, abused. In your grace, make us into a holy people whose priorities and commitments conform to your will.

HOLOCAUST MEMORIAL DAY

God of love and truth,

As we look back upon the enormous genocides of the twenti-eth century, we shudder with horror at our capacity for evil, at the human ability to destroy others in the name of justice. But we shudder because history repeats itself, beating the rhythm of genocide through the centuries and even through the back streets of our civilised world today. And we ask why such atrocities continue.

When we presume that such evil is the exclusive property of a single nation, or race, or generation, or religion, forgive us our pride and awaken us to the realities of our complicity in evil.

When the media allow the reporting of evil atrocities to be eclipsed by fascinating trivia, may the truth be known and the pain be shared.

When governments fail to defend justice because of commer-cial pressure or diplomatic risk, give them wisdom to perceive and courage to act.

When indifference, ignorance or hopelessness silences the prophetic ministry of your church, pour out your Spirit afresh and revive in us a Christ-like compassion.

God of love and truth, in a world where human hearts are so vulnerable to evil, bring your healing touch in all its fullness, beauty and hope.

ALPHA AND OMEGA

Lord God, Alpha and Omega, Beginning and End.

We entrust our lives to you afresh.

Be our beginning. Be our end.

Be our purpose, our energy, our action.

You who invite us to live in the new Jerusalem,

To take our place there because of your love expressed to us on this earth, in our life, in our time.

So may we be ever more fully your people in here and now, as we seek to live the life of heaven on earth.

Inspire our prayers, use us to answer them, be at work to fulfil them.

We pray for those with no view of heaven, without hope, without joy.

For those whose joy has been robbed through broken relationships, through failure, through misplaced trust. Grant them a glimpse of heaven, and an invitation to joy.

For those whose hope has been robbed by forces beyond their control, by war, and hunger and politics. Grant them a foretaste of true justice, and a reason to hope in you.

For those with no view of heaven, may the structures, and relationships that shape this world be challenged and changed. May your people truly live as a sign of hope. Bring justice and righteousness to this earth, Lord God, Alpha and Omega, Beginning and End.

PRESENTATION OF CHRIST

Lord as we consider your coming to the Temple in the vulnerability of a fragile child, open our eyes again the power of your vulnerability in our world today.

We think of Simeon and Anna, awaiting a liberator to free their nation – and seeing no powerful tyrant, no war mongering superhero – but see nevertheless in the fragile child the true nature of your world-changing, life-changing power. And we pray for discernment amongst those who claim to be your people. Forgive us for our blundering inability to recognise the true nature of your power.

Forgive us when see growing ecological calamity, and entrust the stewardship of your creation to powerful people whilst offering only token gestures of ecological greenwash to clear our oily conscience. Show us what it means to encounter you in your vulnerability, and to immerse ourselves in that vulnerability and discover the joy of making a difference.

Forgive us when we see growing economic injustice, and are happy to tolerate it because we live on the right side of the poverty line. Show us again what it means to encounter you, in the hands of an impoverished family, whose penniless character has a greater impact on our world than any great leader. Help us to encounter you in your economic vulnerability, to join you there, and to learn what it means to pray properly for daily bread.

Forgive us when we are happy to inherit our interpretive filters from cultural media with their own story to tell and their own interests to defend. Show us what it means to discern, and to find our place within the narrative of what you are doing in the world – so that we might learn again what vulnerability, and power, and practical, political, ecological and economic salvation really are.

Forgive us, because we fear that had we been in the Temple yearning for a better world, we probably would not have recognised the pathetic, feeble, helpless baby as our means of salvation.

So open our eyes, we pray, that we might immerse ourselves

in the hunger for liberation – and that we might recognise the radically alternative power dynamic with which you confront our world.

By your power, establish the practical peace witnessed by the prophet.

By your grace, reveal to us the ludicrous wisdom of trusting in the pathetic Christ he held.

By your Spirit, may we become a means by which our prayers for the world find an answer.

TRANSFIGURATION SUNDAY

Into the midst of suffering, piercing the shadows, entering our darkness we celebrate the glorious presence of Jesus.

Standing before us with Moses and Elijah, with the laws and the prophets, and your spoken Word, we celebrate the presence of Jesus today.

And we celebrate because in Jesus we see that no avenue of suffering, injustice or loneliness is unknown to him or beyond his reach. And so we pray with confidence in Jesus, for those in our world who must go without food and drink, without family and friendship, without home and without peace.

We pray that in Jesus we may see reconciliation.

In powerful nations whose excessive luxury is distanced from the crippling reality of nations stricken by poverty. May they be reconciled.

Where people have fallen out, refuse to talk because of bitterness, hatred, laziness or fear – perform the mighty act of reconciliation that brings wholeness of life. May they be reconciled.

Where violence brings death and suffering and homelessness

to those with no protection, bring justice for all, and peace for those who must live in fear. May they be reconciled.

Where people have rejected you because of luxury or ignorance, injustice or inconvenience, reconcile the world to yourself, and make us agents your reconciling love.

Loving God, whose glory we see in the unlikeliest of place, bring reconciliation to our world today. Reconcile us with you and with one another. By your loving grace may the world see the Son of God and listen to him.

VALENTINE'S DAY

God of love,
  Teach us how to love one another as you have loved us.
  We pray for those who feel themselves unloved and forgotten.
  Bless them through our prayers and our actions.
  We pray for those for whom a simple act of grace,
  would make a big difference to their lives.
  Bless them through our prayers and our actions.
  We pray for the people we like the least,
  or who dislike us the most.
  Bless them through our prayers and our actions.
  We pray for those we love and who love us. Keep our relationships alive with your love.
  Bless them through our prayers and our actions.
  We pray for those in our world who hunger and thirst and fear. Make your love known to them through government policy and political will.
  Bless them through our prayers and our actions.
  Teach us how to love one another, as you have loved us.

LENT SEASON

At this dark time, as we await the hope of resurrection, we stand before you our God.

We wait, and we hope, and we long for you to act.

We stand before you with fear and doubt,

With concern, with hope, with disbelief, with despair.

But in this time, and in this place,

We nevertheless stand before you.

We pray for leaders, for all entrusted with decisions that affect millions.

For those with the power to change the world for better or worse, we pray that the hope of new life will reach into the corridors of power.

We pray for nations whose inhabitants are trapped in cycles of poverty, hunger and suffering. For people whose future promises no life, and whose past gives little reason for hope.

We pray that the hope of new life will reach into the forgotten agonies of those without hope.

We pray for those concerned about their health, about their mortality, consumed with the pressures of body and mind.

May the promise of new life reach deep into the lives of those who live in fear.

As your people, we stand before you, a sum of all the hopes and all the fears of all the descendants of Eve, and we wait, and we hope, and we long for you to act.

Bring this dark night to an end, and bless our world with the glorious dawn of your resurrection light.

LENT: DESERT PLACES

God of heaven and earth: God who made the universe beyond our knowing and the hairs on our head, we are told to believe that you are everywhere; but so often, and for so many, it feels like you have withdrawn.

For the people facing disasters, for those still hoping for good news of friends and relatives; for those suffering the effects of catastrophe; for those already grieving; for those feeling the effects of hunger and thirst; for all living in a desert from which you have withdrawn.

Come to us, we pray.

For those in war zones; for those living with injustice in occupied territory; for those in regions beyond the gaze or interest of our media; countless places and people, living in a desert from which you seem to be absent.

Come to us, we pray.

For the church and our church; facing pressure from beyond; discord from within, when our churches feel like a desert place from which you have withdrawn.

Come to us, we pray.

For ourselves, our families and friends, when loneliness, fear, shame and anxiety and busyness take root, and you seem to have withdrawn from us.

Come to us, we pray.

Lord, in our world, in our church, in our lives, when it seems to us that you have withdrawn, Make yourself known to us afresh. Make your presence felt anew. Make it true for us, for our church, for our world, that your name is Emmanuel, God with us

Because that is the name in which we pray.

LENT HOPE (Rom 5:1-5; 8:18-25)

God of hope, God of Lent, Show us what it is to follow you to the cross, To follow you to the tomb.

Forgive us for trying to fix the world from a safe distance. Show us what it means to get our hands dirty in the hopelessness and despair to which others are subjected. Show us what it is to join others in their darkness.

For those living in the darkness of poverty, of loneliness, of grief, of fear – move us we pray, to be a true companion. Give us courage and discernment, that we might know:

How best to be alongside those in poverty – so that we truly pray for our daily bread.

How best to be alongside those trapped in loneliness, that our presence might somehow convey your presence.

How best to be with those with grief, so that their tears become our tears, and our hope become theirs.

How best to enter the fear of others, so that we might recognise the darkness in which others live, and remain with them nevertheless. And so may we be mediators of genuine hope.

But grant us also the courage to receive hope when it is offered to us, that we might not wallow in our own sorrow, or despair in the darkness the we face, or cower beneath the fears that haunt us.

Show us how to receive true hope in whatever form you bring it to us.

Show us what it is to inhabit darkness when that is where you lead us, that we might experience real hope when that is what you offer us.

LAMB OF GOD: Lambing Season

Loving God, we come to you in the name of your Son, Jesus Christ, the Lamb of God who takes away the sin of the world.

As we look at the effects of sin in our world, we despair and lack the power to change.

We tell ourselves it will be alright, that you are victorious, that the Spirit will overcome.

But the suffering goes on,

And we feel powerless to change it.

And then we see the powerlessness of the lamb.

So, beyond our imagining, and our natural capacity to hope, may your strength be made perfect in our weakness.

When we see the insanity of trade laws that favour countries like ours, but keep in poverty the millions we will never see – we long for the lamb of God to take away the sin of the world.

When we see governments make rules that seem to widen the gap between the powerful and the powerless, we long for the lamb of God to take away the sin of the world.

When we see your church, preoccupied with secondary issues, and feel our own guilt in doing the same, we long for the Lamb of God to take away the sin of the world.

When we feel ourselves ashamed in your presence, proud in your presence, repulsed by your presence, Lord Jesus, look us again in the eye, Lamb of God, who takes away the sin of the world and our sin.

Show us how to be weak in your presence, in order that your strength may somehow be made perfect here and now.

PASSION SUNDAY

As you take up your cross, give us courage to follow. In the loneliest times, beneath the darkest shadows, through the most terrifying of circumstances, you have gone before us.

Show us what it means to carry our cross, to live a life of sacrifice:

An act of selflessness beckons us,
but we shun it because it is too hard.
Give us your readiness to act.
A desire to give to others something of ourselves seems like the right thing to do,
but we haven't the stomach for it.
Give us your passion to serve.
A letter is waiting be written,
but we would rather do something else.
Give us your loving care.
A difficult conversation awaits us,
but we know we must face it.
Give us your courage.
An offence has wounded us deeply,
And made us bitter.
Give your grace to forgive.
An addiction has gripped us,
But we dare not talk to anyone about it.
Give us your resolve.
A change in our habits we think is important,
But we put it off until tomorrow.
Give us your will.

Give us the courage to take up our cross and follow you, to live a life of self-giving love, that the world might know that we are your disciples. May the oppression and injustice, the violence and the greed, that crushes so many in this world, be defeated today by the cross of Christ. Give us the strength to carry that cross.

FAIR TRADE

Lord we thank you for this world which you created, which you love, and which you are reconciling to yourself.

In a world where unjust global trade laws and unrighteous western consumerism darken the plight of those without influence and without a voice,

Make us a holy people.

Make us aware of the effects of our spending habits,

Make us God-fearing and righteous in the way that we go shopping.

May we worship you not only as we focus on you here today, but as we wander around the shops and tomorrow.

May we seek to please you not only with our praises today, but with our choice of brands tomorrow.

May we honour you not only as we gather here today, but as we pack our shopping tomorrow.

May our spending habits bring health and healing to this world. Forgive us for the part we play in exploiting the distant poor by the way that we shop. Help us instead to support a ministry of true retail therapy, where healing and wholeness are experienced not merely by those who buy, but by those who produce our goods.

In the sweat shops that make our clothes,

Amongst the slaves who produce our chocolate,

On the plantations that produce our coffee and tea,

Bring the light of justice and economic fairness,

By your grace, enable us to live in such a way that may we help and not hinder your work of reconciling the world to you.

FAIR TRADE II

God of justice, we thank you for the fair trade movement, and the difference it has made to countless people throughout the world.

We thank you for work well done, for wages fairly paid, for products getting a fair price. For the life and hope that the fair trade movement brings to whole communities.

We pray also for justice in the way that goods are bought and sold between countries. Where those in power still pay the lowest prices to the poorest peoples in order to boost their own profits. Where the demand of cheap goods for the wealthy, makes life impossible for the poor. Where large companies seek fair trade in a few of its products, but continue to act unjustly in their wider trade deals, we pray for justice.

As the fair trade logo becomes a marketable commodity, we pray that its integrity will hold and that fairness will continue. Especially, we pray for producers of chocolate, coffee and clothes: that through the work of fair trade they will not only receive a better deal than they currently have, but a fair deal.

Lord, we thank you for the way that fair trade promotes healthy relationships between buyers and sellers, and pray that their work will be blessed. May fairness and justice mark all of our relationships, and speak of the righteousness by which your people are to be known.

THE ANNUNCIATION

As we call to the mind Gabriel's announcement to Mary, we consider our receptivity to your will.

May we be ready to hear your Word to us, in whatever form it comes. Whether your word is mediated through a friend or family member, through those we love, through those who threaten or loathe us, through those whom we dislike or detest. Teach us what receptivity to your Word really entails, and help us to ditch the fantasies we tell ourselves about ourselves.

May we be courageous enough to hear your Word when we disagree with it. When it requires more of us than we are willing to give. When it contradicts deeply held convictions. When it compels us to the kinds of actions for which we feel ill-prepared.

May we be hopeful enough to hear your Word when it comes as unexpected encouragement. Ready to abandon all self-doubt and any self-loathing – and ready to engage with your love for us despite our self-perception.

And so may your word to us prove itself as salvation to others, liberation for those who are oppressed, comfort for those who mourn, sustenance for those in need. May your word to us drive us to offer the right kind of care, in the right way, to the right people. Make us so receptive to your living word – that we become its true mediators.

And so grant us, like Mary, the depth of character and strength of insight, to declare readily, 'Let it be unto me, according to thy Word.'

    To the glory of your name.

PALM SUNDAY

God of liberation, we stand before you today with all who suffer because of injustice.

With those who are hungry and thirsty, whose food is stolen by greed, war and famine.

    Lead your people to liberty

    For those who are angry, bitter or imprisoned, because of unfairness.

    Lead your people to liberty

    For those who have given up hope, whose grief has no light at the end of the tunnel, who believe they have been ignored, forgotten or betrayed.

    Lead your people to liberty

    For governments that could make such a difference, but who fail to work for justice

    Lead your people to liberty

    For your church, when it is paralysed by laziness, indifference or fear.

    Lead your people to liberty.

God of liberation, may the glorious light of your Gospel reach into the darkest corners of our world and our lives, and open the eyes of your people's hearts, that we – even we - might embody your compassion, your healing power, and your self-giving love.

EASTER SUNDAY

Lord Jesus, we thought that there is too much evil in the world, and that justice was just a pious dream.

But today you have risen from the dead.

Lord Jesus, we thought that governments and big businesses run the world, carry all the power, hold all the cards. We thought that the little people will always be crushed by them.

But today, you have risen from the dead.

Lord Jesus, we thought that the kingdom of God was being defeated by the forces of hunger and violence and oppression. We thought that the suffering of this world was too great for you to deal with. We thought that maybe you were powerless to change our world.

But today, you have risen from the dead.

Lord Jesus, we thought that so many individuals seem to reject you, that maybe you don't exist outside our imagination. We have sometimes struggled to see you at work in daily life.

But today, you have risen from the dead.

Lord Jesus, we thought that our churches were not very good at being your witnesses. We thought that your kingdom depends on our action. And we thought that we cannot be the people you call us to be.

But today, you have risen from the dead.

Lord Jesus, we thought that there is too much evil in the world, and that justice was just a pious dream.

But today you have risen from the dead.

Lord Jesus, risen from the dead, cause your church to rise and to radiate the new life that is our world's true hope.

EASTER II

God of stability, we thank you for the seasons, for longer days, for warmer son, for blossoming tree.

God of surprises, we thank you for the way you bring to us new life in ways that shake us, disturb us and liberate us.

God of stability, we ask you with confidence for justice in the world.

In the knowledge that the effects of sin break your heart as they break ours.

We pray for hungry and thirsty children, who scratch their living from nothing;

For communities torn apart by war and disaster, who send their days in fear;

For broken and lonely people, who spend their nights awake;

God of surprises, we pray for you to act,

To change these lives,

To change our lives,

To show that here and now, you are at work bringing healing, wholeness and justice.

By your grace, and by your Holy Spirit, may we your people share in this work.

God of stability, God of surprises, we thank you that death does not have the final word, and pray that your people become ever more fully the living proof that Jesus is alive.

SPRING TIME: God of the Seasons

Lord God of all creation – we thank you for the change in seasons.

For the life that floods into the world around us, for the warmth in a sun that has long seemed heatless, for the colours that fill our surroundings with the beauty of Spring, we thank you.

And Lord we pray that our lives may ever flood into the daily wonders of this world, bringing hope and warmth and new life. By your grace, so fill us again with your Holy Spirit, that as sure as day follows night, so too will the presence of your people bring love into our world.

Not sloppy and sentimental love, but practical, political, life-changing, world-making love. Make it true for our world, that as constant and welcome as the seasons that breathe life through this world of your creation – so too, may your church be a source of light and grace and freedom.

God who breathes life into Adam, and new life into the tomb – breathe your life into our church, and into our world – to the glory of your name.

16

Intercessions for Easter Term (May-Sep)

MAY DAY

As warmth returns to the sky and colour to the land, we thank you for the world you have created.

We thank you for the beauty of golden sunrise, budding leaf and good harvest.

But we lament the barren field, the depleted forest, the malnourished child.

We thank you for the beauty of friends, of good relationships, of opportunities for care.

But we lament the damage we have caused to others, the suffering our lifestyles inflict upon those we will never meet, those who have failed because we have succeeded.

We thank you for the opportunities each day brings, for the breath in our lungs and the pulse in our hearts.

But we lament over the time we waste, the people who have little in the way of opportunity, and we pray for those we know, who do not enjoy good health,

God of season, of day, or hour, help each of us to be good stewards of the time, the friends, and the family you have entrusted to our care. Fill us afresh with the Holy Spirit, so that colour and warmth and life flow into our world through the little colonies of heaven you call your church.

THE UNEXPECTED GOD

Lord, we would love to create you in our own image; to share our values and views, to be moved by what moves us, angered by what angers us, to love what we love.

But when you come to us in Christ, you are not what we expect. We cry for liberation – Hosannah – and we pray that you liberate the world in your way.

But we see injustice and violence. In the people of [...] – and as we stand with these people, we cry for liberation and we long for you to act.

We see people in [...], trapped in uncertainty, in grief, in fear. And we stand with these people and cry for liberation.

We see people who we know, imprisoned by bitterness and grief, harbouring resentment and hatred towards others, feeling that [our government] is failing them. And we stand with these people and cry for justice.

CHRISTIAN AID WEEK (Mid May)

Lord God, our Provider.

We worship you as the one who meets our needs, who grants our daily bread, who restores our humanity.

We worship you as the God who knows human need from experience, who knows want, and thirst and humiliation.

And we worship you as your people, in a world where wealth is mixed with poverty; where we have all we need, but don't know how to share. Where want, and hunger and thirst and humiliation are hidden from those with the power to offer challenge and bring change.

So, open our eyes. Not only that we learn sad facts about the world. But open the eyes of our heart, that we may feel our place in this world, as your people.

Where there is need, teach us to learn where our wealth lies, and help us to give.

Where there is injustice, teach us to learn the causes, and help us to fight.

Where there is brokenness, teach us to learn of our own brokenness, and help us to bring wholeness.

Help us to look to you, that we neither remain ignorant of the world,

Nor lose ourselves in despair at its brokenness.

Show us how to worship you,

The crucified God, the risen God, the God who provides.

Help us to carry our cross, to accept your gift of new life, to bring that gift to others.

MOTHERS' DAY (May)

Creator God, we worship you as one who loves us with a mother's love,

And comforts us as a mother comforts her child.

In Christ we see you as the vulnerable child of a teenage

mother: loved and treasured, nurtured and protected, fed and clothed.

And so we thank you for the calling of motherhood, and pray that you would encourage all mothers as they live out their calling. We thank you for the memories they create in our hearts and the selfless devotion they offer. We thank you also for the commitment they show, the compassion they feel and the comfort they bring.

Today we pray for those countless mothers in our world who cannot care for their family as they would wish. For those who feel defeated in the call to motherhood. We think of those who have been unable to provide their children with food, and watch helplessly as poverty and malnutrition take their toll.

We think of those who have been unable to protect their children from the ravages of violence and war.

We think of those who have failed to provide a stable home, and must take to the road to live as refugees for the sake of their children's safety.

Lord we praise you for the unspeakable love that so often flows from mothers even in these darkest of situations, because it points us to the love you show to us.

Move us we pray, to appreciate and support the mothers who live in our home or town, as well as to appreciate and support those who struggle in dangerous, poverty stricken and hungry places. Move us to action, that we might truly be committed to seeing your heavenly love ever-shining through the faces of all you have appointed to represent you as mothers.

ASCENSION SUNDAY

Lord God, it seems strange to us that when we celebrate your ascending into heaven, we celebrate your absence.

So, as we lift our eyes to heaven, help us to be the Body of Christ on earth.

Lord, we long for your spirit to fill our church – that we may be truly present in this world's suffering.

Where parents sift through bins for their family meals; where orphans beg in the street for their food; where compassion is the only source of nourishment,
May your people be present,
And may you be present through us.
Where governments budget for war; where trade laws favour the wealthy; where business is given a vote:
May your people be present,
And may you be present through us.
Where broken relationships crush people; where the death of a loved one stings to the core;
Where loneliness tightens its grip;
May your people be present,
And may you be present through us.
Lord, though you are in heaven,
Do not distance yourself from us.
May we seek your presence in others, hear your voice in others, offer you our love through loving others.

By your Spirit, and by your grace – may the paths of our discipleship be marked by your own foot-prints.

PENTECOST

Lord God, as once your Holy presence filled the temple, on Pentecost we thank you that your Holy Spirit now fills your people the Church.

Fill each of us with your Spirit that our lives are daily transformed from one degree of glory to another.

Ignite in us a passion to seek your will, a desire to know your word, and a readiness to respond.

So fill us with your Spirit that our lives cannot help breathe out your praise.

Make your Church a temple of the Holy Spirit.

Where there is injustice, make your church a royal priesthood and a holy nation.

Where there is violence, make your church an ambassador for Christ.

Where there is greed, hatred or pride, grant your church a truly prophetic voice.

Fill your people with your Holy Spirit, that we might be a holy presence in your world.

PENTECOST II

Spirit of God, unseen but ever active, we praise you for the fruit of your work that we see all around us. From the buds on trees, to the characters changed through the course of time, we see your hand at work. In all we take for granted, in all that fills us with joy, at every meeting of human hearts, we see your hand at work.

Continue your work in our lives, we pray, that your flame may blaze every more brightly within us.

Soften our hearts, help us to listen fully to others, whether they are friends, enemies, words of people we will never meet, stories of people who need our help. Fan the flame of your spirit within us.

Reawaken our desire for service, inspire us to work for justice. In the family, in the nation, across the world. Whether the injustice is a child learning how to play, or a child who will not eat today – make your spirit blaze in our lives and in our church to establish fairness and justice in this world.

Open our beings to true communication. Amongst those closest to us, on whom we depend and who depend upon us. Between brothers and sisters in Christ, between colleagues at work and friends at play. Between a wealthy nation and a broken world. Dwell in the midst of our relationships, so that your fruits blossom into being before our eyes.

Loving, Holy Spirit. Burn within us, make us Holy, strengthen our faith, deepen our love.

INTERNATIONAL CHILDREN'S DAY (June 1st)

God of the present:

Forgive us for our mechanical view of people.

Forgive us: For seeing in young people, only their future; For seeing in old people, only their past; And for seeing in everyone else only one thing or another.

In Jesus we see you being present to children, and children welcomed into your presence.

So open our eyes again to your presence in children.

In the children overfed with junk food, and in the malnourished;

In the children starved of love, in those who know computer games better than they know their parents;

In the children taken as expendable resources – be it as soldiers or sex slaves.

In the children physically bullied by others, or mentally bullied by television adverts and peer pressure.

God of the present – show us how to act and how to live in a world that tolerates injustices inflicted upon those with little voice of their own.

But help us to see, and to hear and to marvel at the unspoken wisdom, the selfless kindness and the image of you, present so clearly and so often among so many children. Help us to seek you, in the children who bear your image no less than anyone else.

Help us to recognise your authority in those for whom we are responsible.

Lord God, whose strength is made perfect in weakness, we thank you for the unseen ministries of children and young people, for your Spirit's work amongst them and for their impact upon the world today.

Show us again, how to come to you as Children.

FATHERS' DAY

On this Father's Day, we pray for all those entrusted with the responsibility of care for others.

For those who, against their will, are distant from their children: we pray for encouragement, for changes in circumstances, and for a means of communication with their children strong enough to allow love to be known.

For those who are distant from their children by choice, by accident, by mistake or by neglect: awaken in them the desire, the hunger, the courage, to become who you have called them to be.

For those who are emotionally distant from their children: grant a renewed vision of who we are in relation to others and to you; give a sense of urgency to arranging life's priorities; grant the courage to admit weakness and passion to passion to work through it.

We pray for all those with a negative taste of fatherhood, whose experience of their own father, leaves them unable to use that word of you.

We thank you for those who find their own well-being, in that of their children – and pray that all our relationships may be fruitful.

We thank you for all those parents who – for the sake of their children - have battled against poverty, against their own selfishness, against tiredness.

We thank you for those who have battled against the divorce industry, against slander, and against despair.

We thank you for all who model what it means to be father.

Open our eyes again to the true burdens and the true joys of fatherhood.

On this day, when we celebrate Fatherhood – may we see in you, the face of one who has struggled with your children, who has felt their failure and felt their joy, and who has never given up on them. And as we look to you, we thank you for all whom you have called to represent you as fathers.

ENVIRONMENT SUNDAY (Early June)

Creator God,

We worship you as the One who creates and re-creates his people.

In a world that is slowly waking up to its duty of care for the creation, slowly becoming aware of the damage we inflict upon the planet, beginning to fear for the future of the earth, let the disturbing truth become ever more clear, in order that a deeper hope may become ever more real.

In a world where talking about our environment fails to result in action, where bold pledges are shallow publicity stunts, where urgent steps are postponed because of their political cost, let our lives reflect our claims in order that our promises ring true.

In a world where guilt or indifference or despair prevent us from being stewards of the creation and worthy heralds of the Gospel, let us worship our Creator in Spirit and in truth, in order that our lives and the life of the world may be remade.

Lord God of heaven and earth, who was creating and is creating, make our lives into signs of hope that point to you, the Creator and Redeemer of the world.

ENVIRONMENT SUNDAY II (Early June)

For the poverty-stricken child who grows up in Southern Asia

May he not lose family and friends when global warming submerges his home beneath the sea.

May he and his children grow up without bitterness towards those who have contributed to the rise in the waters that will devour his village.

May he live to see his relocated grandchildren play without fearing for their future.

For the oil-fuelled child who grows up in the West,

May she never lose her childlike wonder at your creation.

May she learn to treasure the gift of creation without consuming it.

May she grow up in a country that is not afraid to sacrifice its own comforts for the sake of the comfortless.

May neither of them be ashamed by the complacency of our own generation.

May they both have reason to praise you for the beauty of your creation.

May they both become grateful stewards of the gifts and resources entrusted to us by you.

On this Environment Sunday, grant us a healthy awareness of our role as stewards of your creation.

REFUGEES
(World Refugee Sunday, June)

Loving God,

We worship you as one whose own son was a refugee;

We worship you as the God whose people fled slavery in Egypt,

We worship you as the God whose people were dragged into captivity in Babylon.

And we pray for those today who have fled their homes and their loved ones.

Through hardship...

Through disaster...

Through persecution...

Through war...

Loving God, for those whose hearts are as broken as their homes; whose hope has all gone; who find themselves unwelcome wherever they seek help - show compassion.

Show it through us.

Show us what real hospitality looks like when it is a gift.

Teach us how to welcome the stranger in our personal lives and our politics.

Let the glory of your love break through your church and into the structures that govern our society.

REFUGEES II (World Refugee Sunday, June)

God of Exodus and Exile, we worship you as the God of displaced and oppressed peoples. We worship you as the one who lived as a refugee, in radical insecurity, as the God of heaven who – in Christ – had nowhere to lay his head.

Grant that our sense of the world might stretch beyond the institutionalised fantasy worldviews we have come to treasure.

May our knowledge of the world reach beyond the limits of where media points us – that we might see a world where living in a steel container is luxury,

Where risking your life to find refuge in another country is the best option,

Where suicide feels like a reasonable response to personal disaster.

Give us the courage to see the world as it is – and to have a realistic sense of our own agency and power and responsibilities in that world:

Forgive us for seeing only the immediate crisis and not the Social totality.

Open our eyes to the wider context that creates refugees, and of our complicity with forces that create refugees.

Forgive us for judging whether another human being deserves to be one of us, according only to their merits or their failures.

Instead help us to see clearly sheer value of their shared humanity.

Forgive us for measuring others only by their economic status, their financial value, or their value to us.

Help us to be a people who recognise the intrinsic value of everyone made in your image.

Forgive us for reducing human beings to numbers, demoting others from homo-sapiens, to homo-economicus, for dehumanising others

You are the God whose being finds expression above all in the lives those of refugee status – so help us to ditch our liturgical fantasies and worship you as you really are.

TRINITY SUNDAY

Loving God, on this Trinity Sunday, we worship you as the God who has is being in loving communion; whose love is revealed in the relational dynamics of communal life. We worship you as the God of relationship.

We pray for those within our family, community, our peers, those who think, and look and act like us. Show us how to relate well to one another; how to hold one another to account when necessary; how to challenge and to support one another.

We pray for those beyond our community, in a world less safe and less privileged than our own. For those in the war torn provinces where even our imagination cannot travel; for those who hunger on account of invisible economic rules that favour us at their expense; for those whose exposure to grief runs deeper than we can imagine. Open our eyes to those who do not feature within our spectrums of diversity. Show us how to use the resources at our disposal to make a difference to the lives of those we will never meet.

We pray for those we think our enemies, because of their nationality, or their ideology, or their belief structures. Open our eyes to the truth they may bring to us, and the falsehoods of our own that might lead us to exclude them. Show us how to take action that is life affirming, instead of taking offence that is dehumanising.

God of relationship. Of all life, and of each life. By your grace, may we find our place within the relationships that you call us to inhabit, to the glory of your name.

TRINITY SUNDAY II

Father God, to whom we pray
    As children dearly loved by you, help us to share your love with others. Pour your love through our words and actions that they may bring wholeness
    to those we love;
    to those we find it hard to love;
    and to those we deeply dislike.

Lord Jesus, through whom we pray
    As your body here on earth, help us to continue your ministry. Help us to see the world as you see it,
    So that we are angered by that which angers you,

So that we are happy about that which pleases you.
And so that we might be agents of peace in your Kingdom

Holy Spirit, in whom we pray
As a living temple, fill us to overflowing. Anoint us, so that
our words and deeds might prove to be,
Good news to the poor
Freedom to those who are unfairly treated
And vision for those without hope

Lord God, Father, Son and Holy Spirit, as you dwell in loving
communion, make your church on earth a loving community,
the living embodiment of the divine love that is active in this
world.

GRADUATION SERVICE (Thanksgiving)

Let us pray
Lord, today we thank you for our college.
For its founder, Sir David Robinson, and all who committed
themselves to establishing Robinson College.
For its benefactors and all who through their generosity and
on-going commitment enable to college to flourish.
For the staff who have created and maintained an environ-
ment where we have worked and learned and grown.
For the fellows and teaching officers who have educated us,
and hasselled us, and supported us, and given themselves to
us.
For friends we have made here, and the role they will play in
our future.
For all who have helped us to become more fully ourselves.

GRADUATION SERVICE (Intercessions)

Loving God,

We thank you for time you have given us, at this university and this college, and pray that we has been taught and learned and nurtured here would benefit the world at large.

In a world beset with ecological challenges, may skills that have been honed here, find their purpose in bringing techno-logical advance, innovation and insight.

In a world facing economic challenges, may gifts that have been recognized and developed here find their fulfillment in bringing justice, enlightenment and hope.

In a world that challenges who we are and what we treasure, may friendships that have been forged here ripple through our world and our future, fostering openness, fairness, and joy.

By your grace, may the benefits that we have received in this place, benefit the world beyond.

GRADUATION SERVICE (MA Thanksgiving)

Loving God, we thank you for all that we celebrate today,

Memories that shape us, make us smile or laugh, or cringe or weep – but that make us who we are.

We thank you for those whose friendship has been formative but whose company we miss.

We thank you for those who have taught us and inspired us and cared for us – those whose influence upon us and commitment to us, we have only come to appreciate after the passing of time.

Opportunities that have opened up and will open up in the future, because of the place where we have studied, the people from whom we have learned, the work we have invested and the work others have invested in us.

For all your blessings, we thank you, Lord.

INDEPENDENCE DAY (4th July)

God of freedom, God of grace.

God of nation and person,

We praise you for your love at work in our world, for your care for individual and nation.

As we remember today the birth of a nation, we pray for the nations of today that struggle under tyranny.

For those whose governments seem to care little for their own people.

For those governments who idolize their own people, and care little about those of other nations.

For governments who hide their tyranny behind clever words that sound caring.

We pray for international rules of trade, justice and environmental righteousness, that will bring meaningful independence to many in our world today.

Where crippling debts and unregulated trade, keep the powerful in power and the poor in poverty, we cry, O Lord, for independence.

EASTER SEASON

Lord God of life, we thank you for blessings you have poured out on each of us. We thank you for the gift in each day we see, the grace of every breath we draw, the opportunity in every moment we live. Thank you for creating us to live in this time and this space, and show us how to glorify you here and now.

During this Easter season, we reflect upon the fate of millions in our world who share the days in which we live on this earth.

We remember over a billion people living on less than one US Dollar a day;

We remember two billion who have no access to proper sanitation

We remember one hundred million children do not go to school;

We remember ten million children die before the age of 5 from preventable disease.

God of the poor and powerless, we stand before you as citizens of a wealthy and powerful nation, and ask that you would show us how to glorify you here.

We pray for justice and hope and grace, and ask that you would enable us to be agents of justice and hope in the time and the place where you have called us to represent you. By your grace, make us a holy people, attentive to you, that we may live the truth as well as speak the truth.

EASTER SEASON II

Lord, in this season of Easter / Lord of Resurrection, we cele-brate your purposes prevailing, the powers being dethroned, the whole world being in your hands.

But if you have the whole world in your hands − why are there so many children in this world who will eat no food today?

Why will thousands of bullets fly from gun barrels? Why will countless people weep with grief? Why, ifthe whole world is in your hands?

Lead us again into the empty tomb. Open our eyes again, to the darkness and stillness and death that surround us. Give us the courage to see this world as it is, and to see ourselves as we are. Like many, we want to hold on to you when you call us to follow you.

So lead us again into the world as it is, the world you love, the world in your hands.

And may we seek you in others so that we feel what others feel, so that the powers that starve children are challenged, so that governments that use violence unjustly are undermined, so that grief and loneliness and death do not have the final word.

In the quiet, we look at the world around us, in all its darkness and death – and we pray for new life.

Show us how to live and love and be channels of your grace –as though the world really is in your hands.

Summon us again, from the empty tomb, to enter the world as it is, as your witnesses.

If the whole world is in your hands, give us the powerlessness to change it, in accordance with your will.

Lord, in this Easter Season / Lord of resurrection, bring new life and new hope, in our world and in our lives.

BASTILLE DAY (14 July)

Lord where injustice rules, where oppressors are too powerful to be opposed, where governments favour those who command wealth and devalue those trapped in poverty,

we long for regime change.

Where the hungry are kept hungry, where prisoners are denied a fair trial, when peaceful demonstrations are answered with violence, we long for regime change.

In our lives, when forces beyond our control inflict pain upon us, steal our hope, and assassinate us with criticisms; when we do all these things to others because we have not acknowledged you as Lord; in our lives, we long for regime change.

In our church, when we are preoccupied with petty con-cerns,governed by trivia and distracted by that which is not you, we long for regime change. We long for your kingdom to come.

RISEN AND ASCENDED

We worship you as the Lord, risen and Ascended.

As we pray for our broken world, we want to ask you when you will fix everything, when your kingdom will come, when justice will be restored, and you tell us to wait; to wait upon you, to attend to you.

But people are hungry now, thirsty now, people lose their lives in our world now, and you tell us to wait. But for how long? Lord Jesus, risen and ascended, show us where you are now, to join you in what you are doing now. Open our eyes again, to attend to you now, and join you in what you are already doing.

But people suffer from war now. And we're pretty sure, we know what needs to be done, what justice must look like, and still you tell us to wait; to attend to you, to see what you are doing – to catch Your Spirit. Help us to know what you are doing, and to join you.

And people are suffering environmental breakdown now. Peoples lives and livelihoods are being wrecked now. Western greed for biofuel drives poor families from their lands now – and we want you to act, and act now. And you tell us to wait. To wait upon you, and to see who you are and what you are doing, and the miracles you are working. Help us not to fix the world, but to wait on you and so see the world transformed.

Lord, we long for justice, for you to act. By your Spirit, show us what you are doing already, ahead of us, despite us, for us. Forgive our arrogance and help us to listen.

Fill us with your Spirit, Risen and Ascended one, restore your kingdom in our lives, that we might know you more, trust you more, serve you more fully. Fill us with your Spirit that we might wait for you, and in so doing, see you at work, and find ourselves drawn in, to the glory of your name, Risen and Ascended Lord.

HOLIDAY

Lord, as we approach summer breaks of various kinds, we pray for ourselves and for our world.

We thank you for the luxury of holiday, for refreshment and rest from work.

We pray for those whose lives are made harder and busier by long summer breaks, and we pray for those without the luxury of a holiday. May your peace be made known in their daily life.

We think of the damage our travel creates in our world, and we pray for motivation and help in tackling the climate chaos now beginning to engulf the planet.

We pray for those whose holiday will be blighted by the anxiety of what awaits their return.

We pray for health, for all whose holiday is an escape from over-busy or unfulfilled lives.

We pray for justice and fairness for those in our world who scratch a living from the tourist industry.

Lord God of Sabbath rest, make yourself known to us afresh, that all our days may become holy days, to the glory of your name.

INTERNATIONAL YOUTH DAY (August 12th)

Creator God, who brings something out of nothing – we thank you for the way that your character, your power and your love are made known amidst weakness, vulnerability, and powerlessness.

On this International Youth Day, we thank you for the gift of young people in our midst, and in our world. We pray that you help us to recognise the authority of the child, the honest insight of the teenager, the wisdom of youth. Open our ears again to the way that your voice falls from the lips of our young people. Open our eyes to the reflection of ourselves that children offer. Open our hearts again to the responsibilities with which they present us.

We think of the plight of young people worldwide. Of the 7.5 million children who will die needlessly this year, because of simple human apathy. We think of those who receive no education, who are forced to flee their homes because of war, who are malnourished, orphaned and stricken with preventable disease.

Show us what it means to listen well to young people, to see the world through their eyes, to hear your voice in theirs. Show us our responsibilities towards the young people entrusted to our care.

Lord God, whose Son was born of a pregnant teenager, who – as a child – taught experts in the temple, and who never reached middle age, show us who we are as we listen to the voice of youth.

OLYMPICS

Lord as we prepare for the coming of the Olympics, we remember before you all that we celebrate, all that we regret, and all that we must challenge.

We thank you for the way in which nations come together, in which diversity is celebrated, for the ways in which we celebrate not only our national pride, but for the gift of our common humanity.

We thank you that hard work is celebrated, that discipline is seen as a virtue, and that the watching crowds are not only spectators but supporters.

We regret the darker side of the Olympics. Where cities have been less than honest and less than fair, in the way they have treated rough sleepers, in the way they have sold contracts to companies, in the way they have privileged the powerful and marginalised the weak.

In the city whose love of gold has wrought disaster upon millions, teach us again the true meaning of failure and success.

As your church in every age struggles to embody a discipline, diversity and a humanness that reflects your divine character – we ask again to learn who we are in relation to one another and to you. Between individuals, between nations, may your love be made known.

May our support for others: friends and neighbours, enemies and strangers, be driven by your self-giving love for us.

As we watch the games, remind us again of the privilege of the time you have entrusted to each of, and help us to live in the knowledge that we are surrounded by a great crowd of witnesses, to the glory of your name.

PARALYMPICS

Lord as we watch paralympians compete against one another, we marvel again at the wonders of the human body and the human spirit. We see people whose courage and determination have overcome social prejudice, physical limitation and mental discouragement.

We thank you for the stories of daily life that underlies every great achievement and every medal won.

Show us, Lord, what it means for us to be courageous in our daily lives.

Show us what it means to be determined as we struggle with the adversities that face each of us.

Show us how to understand any social struggles we may face, within their proper context.

Lord, in a world where we are so often inspired by the trivial, and heroes are so often mediocre, we thank you that as we watch the Paralympics we see something of what it means to be truly and fully human.

If our human life is a gift that comes to us, if humans are

made in your image – show us again who we are, who you are, and where we are in relation to you.

WORLD HUMANITARIAN DAY (August 19th)

God who loved the world enough to send your Son, today, we pray

For those who risk their lives to help others in times of disaster.

For observers of conflict, who risk their lives to monitor and record injustices in regions of conflict.

For aid workers who have sacrificed their long term comfort to give themselves to helping others in regions of economic and social hardship.

For those working for voluntary organizations because they want to change the way the world works.

In the midst of the suffering in our world, we celebrate those who find joy in helping others.

In your presence, we thank you for those who give themselves to others, for the glimpses they give us of your character, and the inspiration they give for growing in Christ-likeness.

You call us to take up our cross and follow you - show us what it means to live a life marked by both sacrifice and joy.

Fill us again with your Holy Spirit, sharpen our vision of you, strengthen our commitment to you, deepen our love for you.

HIROSHIMA DAY (August 22)

Lord as think about the world which you love, and in which you have called us to live – give us the strength to learn who and where we are.

On this death, give us the grace to stop and consider the horrors of world war, particularly the nuclear explosions that ended the last one.

Lord as we gaze across history to the bleakest moments of our existence, our eyes rest on the horrors of Hiroshima and Nagasaki – the deaths of 200, 000 civilians in a moment, and the agony faced by many more afterwards.

Let us not shrink from the truth of our human readiness to hurt and main and destroy one another – and let us not be overwhelmed by hopelessness to do anything about this.

For the scars that have entered a nation's memory, for our own readiness to hurt others, for our own willingness to justify this to ourselves and to others, we seek your forgiveness.

We ask you for friends-in-Christ who may help us to free ourselves from our self-delusions, and to walk more closely with you.

Where hatred, jealousy and greed lead us as a nation and as individuals, to mistreat others – may we experience a grace that penetrates the bleakest and wildest of human terrors.

Lord, on this day we remember some of the darkest moments in our human history – we realise that darkness breaks out of history and into the present.

Open our eyes again, to the world as it really is – to the reality that every month today more people die of preventable diseases than died Hiroshima.

By your grace, help us to face head-on, the terrors of the world as it really is – so that we may understand who you really are and who you call us to be.

Lord God, who sows seeds of life in the deepest nothingness

of death – bring your disruptive, disturbing, charge of life into the midst of your church, so that we may become ever more fully a source of true hope, a light to the world, an outpost of heaven and an expression of your life-changing love.

BACK TO SCHOOL

God of life and love, we thank you for the new beginning that each day brings.

We pray for the young people who will return to school, for those who are moving school, and those who are attending school for the first time. Eclipse anxiety with excitement, that education may be a truly liberating and joyful experience.

We pray for parents who breathe a deep sigh of late summer relief, and for parents who worry on their child's behalf.

Awaken in them an awareness of the calling of parenthood, and encourage them through the highs and lows of their privileged ministry.

We pray for young people preparing to leave for university.

Equip them with all that is needed on the road to independence. As their parents face a miniature grief, comfort them with the assurance of your presence with them and their children.

We pray for all who long for a new start. Reveal yourself to them as the God whose mercy is new every morning.

You who have promised to restore the years the locusts have eaten, restore to us this day a deep love for you, a renewed desire to please you, a passion to receive the future you have planned for us.

EDUCATION SUNDAY (September)

God of freedom and life, We praise you for the gifts of education, and for those who labour to teach others.

For school teachers and university lecturers, for those who work in toddler groups and nurseries, for parents and grand-parents, for Sunday school teachers, and for those who radiate wisdom without realizing, we thank you. And we ask you that they might be encouraged in their work, and valued for the role they play.

Wherever children are brought up by those with a lust for terror, or by the impersonal face of the digital screen, we pray that you would bring true freedom.

Wherever market forces or nationalism or greed produce adults who have never grown up, we pray that you would bring true freedom.

Wherever people are programmed instead of taught, brain-washed instead of enlightened, manipulated instead of edu-cated, we pray that you would bring freedom.

Teach us to recognize our own role in education, help us to encourage those who have committed their lives to this task, and make us all to heralds of the truth that sets people free.

INTERNATIONAL PEACE DAY (Mid September)

Lord, give us a true vision of peace.

Not a peace that is tranquil, a peace that needs us to put our fingers in our ears to silence the cries of others.

Not a peace that is violent, based upon silencing our enemies by using the sword against them so that we may feel secure.

Not a peace that is lazy, and frees us from the responsibilities of work and struggle and determination.

As we see the horrors that continue to unfold in [...], we want to ask why you seem to do nothing to bring peace.

As we see the endless cycles of violence turning in Israel and Palestine, we want to ask why you – and Almighty and loving God – do not intervene to bring peace.

As we see the indirect violence that our peaceful lives inflict upon those working under conditions of slavery, upon those whose environment is depleted, upon those whose economies are imprisoned in debt – we want to ask why you allow this to happen.

But all too often, our prayers rebound on us. Why do we allow this?

Fill us with your Holy Spirit, that we might truly become a people of genuine peace: a people who fight for peace, a people whose relationships with others are marked with peace; a people whose lives are marked by our relationship with you.

17

Intercessions for Michaelmas Term (Oct-Dec)

THE NEW ACADEMIC YEAR

As we enter this new academic year,
　　We bring before you our hopes and dreams,
　　Our aims and objectives,
　　The best of our intentions and the worthiest of our ambitions.
　　We bring before you all that we hope to make out of this coming year,
　　And submit it all to your life-changing grace.

When our priorities submerge us in pointless tasks,
　　When our ambitions fail us or overtake us,
　　When our hopes seek the fulfilment of none but ourselves,
　　When our hearts deceive us to think that we are right when we are not
　　Lift our eyes from the world under our nose
　　Open our eyes to who you really are.

Open our eyes that we might see the future you have already planned for us.

Grant us:

the courage to seek your kingdom;

the energy to labour where labour is needed;

the wisdom to see when it is not;

the grace to be quiet when we need to listen,

the humility to receive from others,

the compassion to hear and see and love those who nobody wants to hear and see and love.

By your loving-kindness, make us the body of Christ, thriving by the indwelling of your Spirit, bringing glory to the Father.

PRISONS SUNDAY (October)

Lord, come to liberate us.

When we are trapped in prisons that we have made;

and prisons which we have grown into;

or prisons which have grown slowly around us,

Come to us, we pray, and bring liberation,

The freedom you have prepared for us.

And open our eyes and ears and hearts so that when you come,

We recognise you – even when your coming is not what we were expecting.

Make us sensitive to the freedom you bring,

Make us agents of your liberation in the world today,

Make us a people who stand as and alongside those who long to be free,

And teach us how to sing Hosannah.

PRISONS SUNDAY II

God of justice, God of mercy
  We pray for those in prisons in our country,
  Especially for those who feel the pain of fear,disgrace or hopelessness.
  We pray that they may encounter you as the God of love, of grace and of hope.
  We pray for those wrongly imprisoned by injustice, especially for those who endure torment and fear, who suffer beyond the reach of our news headlines, beyond our knowledge and beyond our care.
  May they encounter you as the God who has suffered unjustly, the God of profound empathy and compassion. With them, we cry to you for justice.
  We pray for those angrily imprisoned by bitterness, hatred or distrust for others. Save them from the coffin of their own loathing.
  May they encounter you as the one who floods our lives with grace, loving-kindness and forgiveness for others.
  We pray for those who are unwittingly imprisoned by greed, selfishness and materialism.
  May they encounter you as the God of the outcast, the down-trodden, the marginalized.Reveal to them the true meaning of the cross, that they may encounter the joy of your resurrection life.
  We pray to you, our crucified God and our Redeemer
  For those who are imprisoned, bring freedom
  For those who are without hope, bring salvation
  For those who are bound, bring liberation.
  For the sake of your Holy name.

NATIONAL ADOPTION WEEK (October)

Loving God,

You have adopted each of us into your kingdom,

We pray for all the children who endure difficult family experiences.

Those who have been abandoned or bereaved, abused or neglected.

Those whose best hope for a happy life is to be found with new parents.

We pray also for parents who have been separated from their children,

Those who feel they can no longer cope.

Those who have had no example of good parenting.

Those who have themselves have been unfairly treated or abused.

We thank you for social workers who seek to value children and parents in all circumstances, and for the way that your grace is made real through them.

And we thank you for those who have been willing to adopt,

To commit themselves to children,

To offer costly and genuine love.

Loving God,

We thank you for the gifts of life and love which so often we take for granted.

And as we think of all who suffer because of their family situation,

We ask that you will lead them to the assurance, acceptance and wholeness for which they were created.

And show us, who are here only by your grace, to be the living embodiment of your heavenly loving-kindness in down to earth ways.

HARVEST

Lord of the harvest, we praise you for the world you have created, the food that sustains us, the relationships that nourish us, the love that feeds us.

Lord of the harvest, may the earth be fruitful for all. May its resources be shared fairly, that the horrors of extreme hunger and poverty might come to an end. Where wealthy and powerful nations invest little in justice for the oppressed, may justice take root and blossom into joy for all who share this earth.

Lord of the harvest, may the leaders of this world also become good stewards of the earth. Where greed and selfishness wreck our environment, where the lust for power and the spirit of empire destroy precious lives, bring a hunger and thirst for righteousness, and cultivate a spirit of compassion for others.

Lord of the harvest, may your church be fruitful. May your people be active in seeking justice, to devote heart and mind and possessions to establish your ways on earth. May all people see from the actions of your church, that Jesus is alive. Send us into the world as labourers who, with word and action, will be a living message of good news to all your creation.

HARVEST II (The Parable of the Sower)

Lord, it seems that throughout the whole history of the Christian church, the church has tried to announce good news for the poor and freedom for prisoners and recovery of sight for the blind, trying to proclaim the Lord's favour.

But after two thousand years, there is still no harvest. Children still starve, wars are still fought, power still corrupts, injustice still reigns.

And we want a harvest, we want to see progress, success, achievement, but we still wait for the harvest.

We long for justice, just as the people did for a thousand years. We want you to call time on suffering.

But Lord, free us from inauthentic solutions... Free us from seeing you as the wizard who waves a wand to fix problems.

Show us how to be involved in what you are doing in the world. To discern you at work in the world.

Lord, we see children dying of preventable disease, free us from indifference and despair, open our eyes again to the calling you offer to us here and now, even as we cry for justice.

When we see wealthy and powerful people, seeing trade laws, making financial decisions to protect the powerful at the expense of the poor, save from indifference and save us from despair. to hear your voice and your command, as it comes to us, in the world, here and now.

When we feel, within the church, that things could be so much better, that we have not achieved our potential, when our lives contribute to the injustice of the world even as we ask for justice, open us again to your word, as it comes to us, in the world, here and now.

Sow your seed in our lives, in our church, in our world, and by your grace, open our eyes to the harvest you reap here and now, the secret growth of the seed, here and now, the evidence and the beauty and the freedom, of your kingdom coming, here and now.

DISABILITY AWARENESS SUNDAY (Moveable dates)

Written by Richard Bowers

Thank you, God, for the Church,
  Help us to share fully in the church family.
  We pray for people who are blind:
  Help them to see Jesus.
  We pray for people who are deaf:
  Help them to hear Jesus.
  We pray for people who cannot use their legs:
  Help them to walk with Jesus.
  We pray for people who cannot speak clearly:
  Help them to know that Jesus understands.
  Please help us all to serve you.
  Fill us with the fruit of the Spirit.
  Love, joy, peace, patience, kindness, goodness,
  faithfulness, gentleness, and self-control.
  Lord, hear our prayer. Amen

ANTI-SLAVERY DAY (Mid October)

Lord we pray today for the millions in our world who are forced to work for little or no wage, who labour under threat of violence, and whose lives are still traded as though they were commodities.

We pray for the 2.5 million who are transported into forced labour around the world.

We pray for the 200 million child labourers, half of whom are slaves, sex objects
  or soldiers.

We pray for those children sold into prostitution in our own cities.

Forgive us that we would rather be ignorant than angry. Awaken within us the truth that sets people free.

Forgive us that we would rather enjoy our cheap products, than ask why they are

so cheap. Plant within us, the hunger and thirst after justice.

Forgive us that we would rather accept that the world cannot be changed, than to live out the practical holiness that remakes the world.

Fill us again, with your Holy Spirit.

Open our eyes to the legacies of the past: the horrors of the slave trade that

have resulted in economic inequality, racism, and violence.

Open our eyes to the realities of the present: where the horrors of slavery are swept under the carpet, and the majority are happy to leave them there.

Open our eyes to a vision of the future in which we have proven to our children and grandchildren, that we would not tolerate or ignore the reality of slavery in our day.

Open our lives to you, that the body of Christ may be compassionate as you are compassionate, angered by that which angers you, moved by that which moves you, and active in our world to the glory of your name.

ONE WORLD WEEK (October / November)

Lord God of hosts, who breaks the bow and shatters the spear,
We pray for nations which are threatened from outside, living

in fear of those who seek the power or the excuse to attack.

We pray for nations which are being devastated from within, torn apart by civil war, whose people have lost homes and families, whose children are left without food or drink or peace.

We pray for the nations with power to cause or prevent war; for the leaders who declare their enemies to be 'evil' and themselves to be 'good'; for those who seek knee-jerk military solutions to social and relational problems.

Lord God of hosts, who breaks the bow and shatters the spear –

May those living in the shadow of fear receive true hope.

May those driven by hatred, suspicion or greed encounter living faith.

May those obsessed with protecting their own interests experience sheer grace.

May your people be active peace-makers, locally, socially, politically, globally.

Lord God of hosts, be exalted among the nations.

Be exalted in the earth.

Eradication of world poverty

Lord God, our Provider. We pray for those in our world who are suffering from extreme poverty.

For the billion people who have never learned to write,

For the hundreds of millions who are malnourished,

For the tens of thousands of tiny children who die every day,

Take us beyond statistics and the guilt they can create.

Save us from compassion fatigue, that we might not become weary in doing good.

Show us your face in the mother desperate to feed her

children, in the flea ridden child with the bloated stomach, in the old man whose life has been spent working for next to nothing.

Show us how to honour you with our resources,

With time and money, energy and education,

May all that we have and all that we are become an act of worship to you that would bring,

Discomfort to the selfish,

Challenge to the political structures,

Encouragement to those who work for justice,

A voice for those who are unheard,

Hope to the oppressed,

Good news to the poor.

SUFFERING CHURCH SUNDAY (Early November)

Lord, you never promised your people a life free from suffering.

You never promised your church a mission free from persecution.

You never promised us an easy path to walk as we follow you.

In our comfortable land, where we can mistake social embarrassment for persecution, and where we so easily romanticise the virtue of being persecuted, we pray for those who today will face a martyr's death because of their love for you.

We pray for those who live in fear, simply because they have chosen to follow you.

We pray for those who have been forced to choose between you and their family.

Where the church faces persecution and hardship, suffering and even death,

May the church also be so filled with your Spirit that they might cope with all the difficulties that face them.

Move us, we pray, to work for a world in which the horror of all persecution is challenged by the demand for justice.

Help us to offer practical support to those who find themselves in need because of religious and political persecution.

And allow us to see your face in the suffering church, to be challenged by their faithfulness, to learn from their love for you.

SUFFERING CHURCH SUNDAY (Early November)

Lord, you never promised your people a life free from suffering.

You never promised your church a mission free from persecution.

You never promised us an easy path to walk as we follow you.

In our comfortable land, where we can mistake social embarrassment for persecution, and where we so easily romanticise the virtue of being persecuted, we pray for those who today will face a martyr's death because of their love for you.

We pray for those who live in fear, simply because they have chosen to follow you.

We pray for those who have been forced to choose between you and their family.

Where the church faces persecution and hardship, suffering and even death,

May the church also be so filled with your Spirit that they might cope with all the difficulties that face them.

Move us, we pray, to work for a world in which the horror of all persecution is challenged by the demand for justice.

Help us to offer practical support to those who find them-selves in need because of religious and political persecution.

And allow us to see your face in the suffering church, to be challenged by their faithfulness, to learn from their love for you.

DIVINE BULLYING (Anti-bullying week: November)

God of fragility and power, God of severity and love,

May your people reflect your image in this world.

We want to ask why humans made in your image resort so naturally to bullying others, and we pray for all victims of bullying.

When we see the most vulnerable members of society manipu-lated and exploited.

When we see those with no public voice removed from their land, be it in Indonesia or North Dakota.

When we see victims of war, footage too hard to film and too hard to watch, of vulnerable families bombed and frightened, displaced and ignored. For all who clawing their way out of the rubble of heartless political decisions, we want to ask you how a loving and all-powerful God can allow this.

When we see those who have been or are being bullied at school, carry their scars into later life. When bullying happens behind closed doors or beneath the radar of our perception. When power we subconsciously wield, blinds us to our complicity in bullying. We want to ask you for the restoration of your true image in our lives.

When we justify our own coercive behaviour by appealing

to some higher power, some greater good, some redeeming ends, some divine name, some isolated sacred text – forgive us, forgive us when our all-too-human words about you, drag your name into the dirt.

And may we discover you afresh, as a God whose power is so radically holy that it cannot be employed for the purposes of human coercion.

May we worship you as a God whose name has always been associated with the marginalised and the outcast and the bullied:

with the beleaguered nation of Israel;
with the outsider status of the prophet;
with the crucified figure of Christ.

And in holding the gaze of this Christ – may the bully and the bullied find themselves renewed and restored in your divine image, revealed to us in the crucified and risen Lord.

REMEMBRANCE DAY (Psalm 46)

Loving God,

Today we remember all those who have died in war.

We remember soldiers who have given their lives, suffered physical injury or witnessed unspeakable horror.

We remember all who have lost homes, and livelihoods and loved ones, because of war.

We remember helpless victims, whose memory is drowned in an ocean of statistics.

We remember,
We look to you,
We ask 'why'?

We ask where you were.

But we see your face
In the fear of the soldier and the despair of the victim.
In the broken child and the bereaved parent.
In the peace campaigner and the reluctant general.

Awaken us to fight the battles that avert war.
Inspire us to disarm our enemies of hatred,
Forgive us for investing in the tools of war,
Liberate us from the lust for security,
Open our eyes to the true depths of horror in our world, that
we may see a deeper hope.
O God, who breaks the rifle, who shatters the missile, and
burns the tanks in fire.
Be exalted among the nations
Be exalted in all the earth.

REMEBRANCE DAY II

Lord God of hosts, we worship you as the God in whose name countless armies have marched and endless battles are fought. And in our world of growing violence and unrest, we pray for peace.

We lament that each new generation must learn the art of peace for itself, only after it has suffered the ravages of war. And we want to remember well.

We lament the deaths of those who have fought in wars, at the end of which we see so little lasting peace. And we want to remember them.

We lament the victims of war who no one misses: for those whose lives are only known to us as statistics. And we want to remember them.

We lament that so often, the only lessons we learn from war – are how to disguise our own nation's violence, how to fight wars by proxy, how to hide casualty lists and civilian deaths.

We lament the power that defence industries can hold over governments.

We lament that war is so often declared long before it becomes a final option.

We lament that those who work to prevent war are rarely celebrated as heroes.

As we remember those who have given their lives in war, those who have lost their lives in war, and those whose lives have been forever damaged by war, we cry for peace – and ask that by your grace, you will make us agents of peace.

A SOLDIER'S PRAYER

We remember those we have sent to fight our wars,
   We think of those who have not returned,
   And we pray for those who have.
   For those who suffer the aftermath of war:
   For those who have died in Road Traffic Accidents, because they had learned they were invulnerable.
   For those who have taken their own lives, because they had learned they were not.
   For those who fear the rage than can overtake them at any moment, and who long for the peace that never can.
   For those alienated from others, because they are alienated

from themselves.

For those haunted by wounded memories that echo through long years,

And tormented by vivid images of ancient trauma.

May we help them to conquer their past, to remain present with them when inconsolable, to offer hope for a future that is not a fantasy.

May we become part of the narrative in which God-given time is restored to them.

CHRIST THE KING

Sovereign Lord, maker of heaven and earth, we worship you as the God of power, whose son Jesus Christ reveals himself to us as king.

In a world of sin, where democracies are so easily corrupted, and dictators are rarely benevolent, we look to you, to your pattern of kingship, to see how the world might work in ways that bring justice and fairness for all.

We lust for power, thinking we can then wield it to build a better world,

But yours is the path of powerlessness, the crown of thorns, the cross-bearing walk-of-shame.

We rush into bringing justice with violence, be it with a nation's armies or with an individual's words of spite,

But in your hands we see no sword-hilt, no pistol-grip, only the nails of a cross.

We measure wealth with coins and bank balances, and convince ourselves we need money to build a better world.

But in you we see wealth in how much we need rather than

how much we have. In you, our King, we see the world turned upside down by self-giving love.

Lord, where our world is driven sour by the lust for power, be it at home, at church, at the work place, or in our governments – free your people from bitterness and frustration, fill us with a life-giving spirit so that all people may see the world changed by the kind of power that grace alone can bring.

Where we barely notice the violence we bring upon others, when we are blinded from our own rage – show us again the king who – when faced with the mocking of an angry mob - was silent, like a sheep before the shearer.

Where greed drives us, consumes us, deceives us – open our eyes again to see how the crowds, the religious leaders, the political authorities – all were brought up short when faced with the peasant builder from Nazareth.

Christ the King, make us humble enough to be agents of your self-giving, grace-filled, life-changing, world-making power.

ADVENT

Advent God, who was and is and is to come, we pray for the world in which Jesus walked and to which he will return.

Our world has never overcome the injustices and oppression, hatred and bitterness, violence and war. As we picture the innocent victims we would rather not see,

Lord God Almighty, who was and is and is to come, come into our world and make all things new.

We praise you for all the good things in our churches that truly reflect your character, but we know there is much in us that needs to change. If we have been taken captive by the spirit of the age, if we have failed to listen to you, and lost our prophetic voice,

Lord God Almighty, who was and is and is to come, come into our church and make all things new.

We thank you for the joys and the fulfilment that accompany your gift of life, but we pray for those who know no joy, and only despair – especially as we face Christmas. Make us a people of grace, a people whose lives are truly a gift to others. Lord God Almighty, who was and is and is to come, come into our lives and make all things new.

Advent God, transform this world we pray, and start with me.

ADVENT II

We celebrate you as the God who comes to us, even as we are busy building our own futures.

We see injustice and war, and we want to forge a future of justice and peace.

We see decline in numbers in churches, and we want to forge a future of growth and success.

We see climate chaos, and want to forge a future of respect for creation.

We see some grow wealthy at the expense of those sinking into poverty, and we want to forge a future of fairness.

We hear the call for a Big Society, but seek a future of true community.

As we look in despair at the suffering in our world and, even now, we long for your coming.

Give us the courage to pray what we say so lightly: Even so, come, Lord Jesus.

ADVENT III

For unto us a child is born, unto us a son is given: and the government shall be upon his shoulder: and his name shall be called Wonderful, Counsellor, The mighty God, The everlasting Father, the Prince of Peace. (Isaiah 9:6)

Advent God, we long for your coming – for your coming into our world where there is so much unfairness, injustice, lovelessness and violence. Save us from the rose-tinted spectacles with which we like to comfort ourselves at Christmas. Open our eyes again to see the world as you see it.

We pray for economic fairness in our world. Where broken banking systems are patched up but not reformed; where gatherings of the nations' leaders seem unable to see beyond bringing more-of-the-same; where one half-baked solution after another after another seems destined to failure: we long for the presence of the Wonderful Counsellor.

We pray for governments and politicians, so often powerless to overcome the will of those with wealth or position, powerless to confront mighty corporations and business interests. In a world where the wealthiest one percent can afford to avoid paying tax, while the poorest help to subsidise them, we pray for justice in governments –and a vision that extends beyond the next election. Where our governments and politicians are powerless to bring justice, we long for the presence of the Mighty God.

We pray for fatherless children – half the children in our poorest countries, and a quarter of them in our wealthiest. We pray for those who have lost fathers, and those whose fathers have abandoned them.

As we stand with these children, we long for the presence of the Everlasting God, we pray for those who have seen too much war: For those who have lost homes and loved ones over pointless conflict, brought about by thinly veiled stupidity, greed or blood lust. When our world seems set to tear itself apart – in petty squabbles; in acts of terror; in declarations of war: we long for the presence of the Prince of Peace.

Silence

But unto us a child is born, unto us a son is given: and the government shall be upon his shoulder: and his name shall be called Wonderful, Counsellor, The mighty God, The everlasting Father, The Prince of Peace.

Lord, if this is you – make yourself real to us.

Make yourself known through us.

Make yourself at home in our lives.

Make your presence felt in our world.

Come, Lord Jesus.

NATIVITY SCENE

Lord we pray for the world in which we live, and which God loves so

much he sent his only son:

When in our governments, in our church, in our lives – we become so obsessed with power that we mistreat other people, Help us to see you, the king of heaven, as the fragile infant in a feeding trough.

When the poor and powerless people of our nation and

our world, are ignored or exploited, Help us to see the mere shepherds who are invited to witness a royal birth.

When so-called experts in finance, in politics, in business, offer solutions to fix our world, but only seem to make things worse – Help us to see the wise men bow before a vulnerable child.

When we fear the melting ice sheets, the changing environment, the chaos in our climate – help us to see the creatures, looking to Jesus as their hope.

When we feel powerless, helpless to change the world, unable to bring fairness, frustrated because we are too little to make a difference, help us to see see the angels of heaven celebrating the fragile child in a peasant's dwelling.

As we celebrate Christmas – reach into our world, our church, our lives in new ways, and by your grace, help each of us to be humble enough, small enough, powerless enough, vulnerable enough, to become your gift to others.

CHRISTMAS EVE

Loving God, giver of life and creator of love,

We pray for those who have no gifts to open this Christmas, for parents who will struggle even to feed their children, for children who will have little reason to smile. May we who celebrate Christmas, become agents of Good News for them.

We pray for those who do not look forward to this time of year, because of family circumstances, difficult memories and loneliness. Lord Jesus, who came into our world, be close to them. May we who celebrate Christmas, truly represent you to those on our own doorstep.

We thank you for the reminders of Christmas, for the truth that you have made yourself thoroughly at home in our midst, that we may call you Emmanuel, God with us. Keep us conscious of your loving and living presence, and make us channels of your grace, not just on Christmas Day, but every day. May we and the church in which we worship become ever more truly God's gift to the world.

CHRISTMAS DAY

Lord Jesus Christ,
On this Day we thank you for coming to earth, to live as one of us.
We thank you for all the presents we have unwrapped.
We thank you for the gifts we have been able to send.
We thank you for the happiness this day brings,
And for all the good food we are ready to tuck into.
But we pray for those who are less happy about today,
For those who are hungry or lonely, away from home or sad, ill or unhappy.
Be near to them, and show us how to be as loving and caring,
As the Jesus whose birth we celebrate today.

CHRISTMAS

In a world where we are told to tighten our belts, endure the recession, brave the financial storm,
Here you are, God with us.
In a world where the gap between rich and poor is ever

widening,

Here you are, God with us.

In a world where so many face a future empty of hope and full of despair,

Here you are, God with us.

In a world where so many are refugees, as you once were, separated from loved ones and from family by miles of impossible journey,

Here you are, God with us.

In a world where loneliness is commonplace, where the sace between individuals is ever widening,

Here you are, God with us.

In a world where we are taught to be dissatisfied with the present, when our satisfaction is always hiding around the next corner,

Here you are, God with us.

In a world where so many, including ourselves, have forgotten you, ignored you, turned our back upon you,

Here you are, God with us.

In the form of a baby in a feeding trough, promising to bring down the mighty from their thrones.

Here you are, God with us.

CHRISTMAS II

Loving God, giver of life and creator of love,

We pray for those who have no gifts to open this Christmas, for parents who will struggle even to feed their children, for children who will have little reason to smile. May we who celebrate Christmas become agents of Good News for them.

We pray for those who do not look forward to this time of year, because of family circumstances, difficult memories and loneliness. Lord Jesus, who came into our world, be close to them. May we who celebrate Christmas, truly represent you to those on our own doorstep.

We thank you for the reminders of Christmas, for the truth that you have made

yourself thoroughly at home in our midst, that we may call you Emmanuel, God with us. Keep us conscious of your loving and living presence, and make us channels of your grace, not just on Christmas Day, but every day. May we and the church in which we worship become ever more truly God's gift to the world.

18

Intercessions by Theme

ART (Picture Language)

God of revelation, who remains unseen – in Jesus we see an image of the invisible God.

In this world, may we become an image that draws attention to you.

Help us to reflect your beauty, your holiness, your grace, your readiness to be involved.

When we keep suffering at arm's length, help us to speak with those for whom no-one has time, to listen to those who might otherwise remain unheard. God of time and space, who became human in time and space, show us how to become human in the fullest sense. That our humanity might draw attention to your divinity.

When we prefer to pray for the poor, rather than become poor – show us the poverty of our worship. Help us to share the plight of those with nothing, so that when we pray for *our* daily bread, we mean it. God who was wealthy, but for our sake became poor – show us how to become poor so that we may discover true wealth.

When we prefer not to know, because of all that is threatened by true knowledge, when we retreat from facts that reveal our cowardice and threaten our comfort – release us from our precious ignorance. God who knew Adam, and covenanted with Israel, grant us true knowledge of our world – in all its beauty and shame – that we might truly discover our God-given place within it.

God of hiddenness, God of revelation – fill us with your Spirit, that we might become an accidental if fleeting image, of the invisible God, to the glory of your name.

CONFLICT I

God of glory, and god of humility

We pray for the world in which your glory and your humility are inseparable.

Because when we look at the world, we see power winning out over humility, we see the powerful oppress the powerless, we see the inescapable truth that might is right.

So we want to ask you why the people of the Ukraine are living in fear of powerful neighbours, and why suspicion and hostility tear their way through an anxious population.

So we want to ask you why the people of Syria no longer bother to cry to the international community for help.

And we want to ask you why with our democratic convictions, our economic policies continue to favour the wealthy, and penalize the disposable humans beyond our privileged circles.

And we want to ask you why our advanced civilizations, are grossly incapable of making sane and sensible ecological policies.

And we want to ask you why it is so easy to hurt and be hurt by those we love.

And when we bring these questions before you, we don't want the smug answers of an aloof deity, or the deified echo of our own makeshift wisdom.

Confront us with who you are, not concealed in beautiful humility of Christ, but revealed in the stark humiliation of the mutilated corpse of the political criminal that is your son.

By your grace, may we find the courage embody your humility as Christ did, the Christ whose humility led him to the shame and failure, and utter defeat of the cross.

And by your grace, make it true, that the resurrection is good news, here and now, good news to those for whom we pray, and good news in the lives of those who seek to worship you. Make it true for us, that your glory is manifest through our bitter humility.

CONFLICT II (Written for Ukraine)

We think of those who have lost what we could not face to lose.
Who face horrors we can barely imagine,
We think of those who queue for food and water and shelter.
We think of those lined up at border crossings.
We think of those separated from loved ones.
Not knowing if, and when they might see them again.
We think of those who could not get out.
Of those trapped in towns that have been surrounded.

Trapped in basements with no light or water.

We think of those who last week had never heard a bomb explode,

And have now become desensitized.

Of those who have seen parts of their neighbourhood where last week they visited shops and talked in the street,

Reduced now to rubble.

We think of those who find themselves with a gun in their hands for the first time.

Who have learned the smell of oil and sulphur, and the kickback of a rifle,

While tanks queue to enter their cities.

We think of those with No shelter. No toilet. No prospect of when this will end. No sense of a solution.

We think of those with the power to change these dreadful circumstances.

We are made aware of the disgusting finitude of our mortality. That hideously insignificant nano-fragment of time in which we the life we live comes and then just goes.

We ask if our life, if all lives, are worth something after all.

And if all lives are worth something, then naturally we long for all lives to be valued. For the people of Ukraine to be valued. And so we long for peace. Real, and political, and hard won peace. Peace above all.

Where there has been the rumble of tanks, the droning of helicopters, the booms of explosions, the snap of gunfire.

Peace, where there has been chaos. Peace where there has been war. Peace for the people of Ukraine.

May we be compelled to use whatever resources have been entrusted to us, to help bring about peace.

CONFLICT III (Written for Ukraine II)

Lord we pray for the people of Ukraine,

When we watch from a distance, free from the illusions of good vs evil and open our eyes to the nature of war, how wars come about, and how wars can be ended.

When world leaders hide behind artificial sympathies, and fake impotence. When they call for prayer as an alternative to bold economic and political action, help us to hold our leaders to account.

When tribalism establishes itself through 'us and them' narratives, may we find others who hold us to account.

But above all, we pray for those who simply want to survive, to escape, to drink, to eat, to be warm, to find a toilet.

For those taking refuge in neighbouring countries, living with radical insecurity and not knowing the whereabouts of their loved ones. Show us how to use the resources at our disposal to offer practical help.

For those trapped on roads and railways, desperately trying to flee westwards, but thwarted at every turn, show yourself to be the God of salvation, of liberation, the God of Exodus.

For those families trapped in cities, seeing the flash of a bomb and waiting for the noise, for those wondering whether the next missile will land on them, be something more than a delusion or distraction or false comfort. Be real.

For those civilians who have taken up arms for the first time, who have never stripped a rifle, or smelt the oil and sulphur or felt the kickback of gunfire. May their defiance and their courage, yield its fruit long before they have to squeeze a trigger or hear the crack and thump of incoming bullets.

God of peace. Make your peace known. Make it known

through us, among others. And so make us worthy of the prayer you taught your disciples, and which we now pray together.

THE DEVIL

Lord God, Creator and Redeemer,

If the greatest trick the devil ever pulled, was convincing the world that he does not exist, help us to recognise the mechanics of evil in our world today: in the invisible hand of the market; in the convincing fair face of the oppressor and the warmonger; in the toxic conviviality of neoliberal ideologs.

When the devil offers shortcuts that offer the fruits of justice, that do not engage with the groundwork of cultivating real justice. Show us what it means to be faithful to you.

Instead of expecting you to turn stone into bread – awaken us to the poverty on our doorstep, where here in Cambridge some people can afford only one meal per day. Teach us not to pray for them until we have taken practical action.

Instead of bowing before the devil, making ourselves be-holden to secular systemic unfairness, as prerequisites for doing your will on earth – help us to trust in your ability to work through those with no power, no financial backing, no social cache. Show us how your strength is made perfect in weakness.

Instead of leaping from the Temple, of assuming your bless-ing on our well meaning objectives – show us what it means for all of our good intentions as well as our bad, to be exposed. Forgive us when our vision of you, our sense of justice, our belief of fairness, is nothing other than a fantasy we have invented to feel good about ourselves.

May your goodness and beauty and truth nevertheless shine through our weakness and failure and delusion. That by your grace, we may nevertheless become more than we are, to the glory of your name.

ECONOMICS I (Global Poverty)

If it matters to you, does it matter to us?

If you hear the cries of the poor, help us to do the same.

If you see the effects of injustice, help us to do the same.

If you act to change the plight of those in dire need, help us to do the same.

Because we suffer compassion fatigue

We can no longer watch disturbing reports on our television

We must turn our eyes from images of children's distorted by hunger.

We don't want to turn our eyes, but there seems so little that we can do.

Forgive us,

Restore to us the hope of the Gospel

Revive in us a passion for justice

Move us to act.

May we be a Gospel people

May our worship and our commitments and our priorities

Become signs that your Kingdom is coming.

Change the plight of those in chronic poverty,

And make us a means by which our prayers are answered.

We worship you as Lord of heaven and earth

So may we see your Lordship change the lives and the plight and the future of those trapped in poverty today.

God of exodus, by your grace, enable us to perpetuate the myths that bring freedom where has been none. To find our place in narratives of liberation, that reflect something of who you are.

God of liberation, we stand before you today with all who suffer because of injustice and oppression.

With those who are hungry and thirsty, whose food is stolen by war and greed and famine.

Lead your people to liberty

For those who are angry, bitter or imprisoned, because of unfairness.

Lead your people to liberty

For those who have given up hope, whose grief has no light at the end of the tunnel, who believe they have been ignored, forgotten or betrayed.

Lead your people to liberty

For democratic governments that could make such a difference, but who quietly make themselves accountable to forces that generate injustice.

Lead your people to liberty

For your church, when it is paralysed by laziness, indifference or fear.

Lead your people to liberty.

God of liberation, may the glorious light of your Gospel reach into the darkest corners of our world and our lives, and open the eyes of your people's hearts, that we – even we - might embody your compassion, your healing power, and your self-giving love.

ECONOMICS II (Debt and Forgiveness)

God of freedom, of liberty, of forgiveness in all its fullness – we worship you as fallen people in a fallen world.

Forgive us for compartmentalising your gifts to us – forgive us for judging people according to their economic status, for our lack of grace in relating to others, for separating spiritual truth from practical reality.

In a world submerged in so much debt, show us what it means to be a people who live and breathe forgiveness.

Where we are ignorant of the harsh realities faced by others, open our eyes to the world as it is. Help us to measure the health of our community, by the plight of its weakest members.

Where we are happy to admire the wealthy because they are wealthy, or to hate them because they are wealthy: liberate us from self-righteousness, jealousy, smugness and bitterness, and help us to inhale grace, and to walk in your footsteps.

Where we mistake greatness for success, where we measure wealth by how much we have, rather than by how much we need, reveal to us the nature of true riches, of the wealth that catastrophe cannot threaten.

Where people feel and are made to feel worthless because they are not creditworthy – help us to embody a different vision of what it means to be human.

Fill us with your Spirit, that we might live in accordance with the Spirit of Jubilee. That our vision of you, would eclipse the false utopias we have learned to treasure. That our commitment to you might spring from every dimension of our being. To the glory of your name.

ENVIRONMENTAL CONCERN I

In a world where eco-fatigue seems to set in before the world has fully awoken to its plight, show us what it means to live well. To live in the light of those with whom our lives interweave. To awaken more fully our relationship to those who may suffer indirectly but unavoidably from our lifestyle. To listen more fully to voices that have been silenced. To grow in awareness of the living world under our nose.

Give us the courage to face disturbing realities, without despair.

In order that genuine hope may become ever more real.

In a world where talking about our environment fails to lead to serious action, where bold pledges can be shallow publicity stunts, where urgent steps are postponed because of their political cost, let our lives reflect our claims.

In a world where guilt or indifference or despair prevent us from treating one another well, enable us to hear the whole creation groan.

Lord God of heaven and earth, who was creating and is creating, make our lives into signs of hope that point to you, the Creator and Redeemer of the world.

ENVIRONMENTAL CONCERN II

Creator God, we worship you as the One who creates and re-creates his people.

In a world that is slowly waking up to its duty of care for the creation, slowly becoming aware of the damage we inflict upon the planet, beginning to fear for the future of the earth, let the disturbing truth become ever more clear, in order that a deeper hope may become ever more real.

In a world where talking about our environment fails to result in action, where bold pledges are shallow publicity stunts, where urgent steps are postponed because of their political cost, let our lives reflect our claims in order that our promises ring true.

In a world where guilt or indifference or despair prevent us from being stewards of the creation and worthy heralds of the Gospel, let us worship our Creator in Spirit and in truth, in order that our lives and the life of the world may be remade.

Lord God of heaven and earth, who was creating and is creating, make our lives into signs of hope that point to you, the Creator and Redeemer of the world.

ENVIRONMENTAL CONCERN III

For the poverty-stricken child who grows up in Southern Asia
May he not lose family and friends when global warming submerges his home beneath the sea.

May he and his children grow up without bitterness towards those who have contributed to the rise in the waters that will devour his village.

May he live to see his relocated grandchildren play without fearing for their future.

For the oil-fuelled child who grows up in the West,
May she never lose her childlike wonder at your creation.

May she learn to treasure the gift of creation without consuming it.

May she grow up in a country that is not afraid to sacrifice its own comforts for the sake of the comfortless.

May neither of them be ashamed by the complacency of our own generation.

May they both have reason to praise you for the beauty of your creation.

May they both become grateful stewards of the gifts and resources entrusted to us by you.

LISTENING

Lord we praise you as the God who speaks, and ask that you show us what it really means to hear.

Show us what it is to hear real in such a way as we might be changed by the encounter.

Show us how to hear the needs that so often bubble up under our own noses – and show us how to respond well.

Show us how to hear those we love, and not take them for granted.

Show us how to hear human need at a global level, and to have a sense our ability to act and respond with whatever power is at our disposal.

Show us how to hear the human need on our doorstep, and how to roll up our sleeves and offer practical help.

Show us how to hear those whose voices are all too often ignored, so that marginalised folk, and outsiders, might be affirmed, and welcomed, and included, and valued.

Show us how to listen to the living world, so that we might play our part in the ongoing struggle for ecological and economic justice.

Show us how to listen to you, so that we might become aware of something bigger than ourselves, and find our own place in wild and life-giving harmonies that transcend our time and our context.

Show us how to listen, so that we might have something to say.

OUTSIDERS I

We worship you as the God of high heaven who makes himself at home with the scum of the earth, whose beauty is revealed in the midst of the world's worst ugliness.

God of the outsider, and the xenos, and the unperson. God of the invisible – show us what it means to engage with the Other.

We thank you for those people who have seen us when we have felt invisible. For those who have welcomed us when we were outsiders. For those who have fed us when we were hungry.

When human lives are reduced to numbers, awaken us to the stories behind the tragedies we see. Especially we think this week of those who died on the fishing boat disaster of Greece. The victims of economic injustice and people smugglers, whose stories are unlikely to be heard. Show us what it means to be a good citizen at a time of international refugee crises.

We think of the invisible people on our streets here in Cambridge, and pray for courage to engage with these people in a way that is consistent with the worship we offer you today.

We think of those closer to home, for whom a comforting word, or a discomforting conversation, may be a vehicle of grace, and recognition, and welcome. Show us how to listen to those closest to us, whose presence we so often take for granted, and whose concerns we may wrongly assume to have understood.

Broaden the limits of our diversity, deepen the roots of our solidarity, strengthen the dynamics of our community.

OUTSIDERS II (Woke Jesus)

Loving God, Almighty and intimate,

We pray for those who do not belong to our own in-group.

For refugees who are not the right kind of refugees, whose ethnic origins see European borders close to them, while remaining open to others. Awaken us to the realities of our selective welcomes, and show us what to do about it.

For those whose suffering does not make it into the media we consume. May our worldview be formed by a willingness to hear the genuine outsider – and by responding to their appeals to us, and their claim on our privilege.

For those whose religious affiliations we find ignorant, half-baked or repulsive. Bless them, we pray. And may we hear something of your wisdom in their belief.

For those individuals who have been vilified without being heard. For people we prefer to hate than to hear. Those we have learned to demonise because of how others have already branded them.

For those we meet only when they deliver our takeaway, or wash our car, or pack our shopping. May their humanity be more visible to us, than the service they provide for us.

For those whose personal struggles we do not understand. Give us the courage to inhabit the stories of others, to become part of their story, to allow them to become part of ours.

For our churches, our communities, and for this college. May our life together remain worthy of the values we treasure. May we be worthy of the flags we fly and the claims we make. May the relationships formed in this place, bring life to the world beyond this place.

OUTSIDERS III (Children)

God of the present:

Forgive us for our mechanical view of people.

Forgive us: For seeing in young people, only their future; For seeing in old people, only their past; And for seeing in everyone else only one thing or another.

In Jesus we see you being present to children, and children welcomed into your presence.

So open our eyes again to your presence in children.

In the children overfed with junk food, and in the malnour-ished;

In the children starved of love, in those who know computer games better than they know their parents;

In the children taken as expendable resources – be it as soldiers or sex slaves.

In the children physically bullied by others, or mentally bullied by television adverts and peer pressure.

God of the present – show us how to act and how to live in a world that tolerates injustices inflicted upon those with little voice of their own.

But help us to see, and to hear and to marvel at the unspoken wisdom, the selfless kindness and the image of you, present so clearly and so often among so many children. Help us to seek you, in the children who bear your image no less than anyone else.

Help us to recognise your authority in those for whom we are responsible.

Lord God, whose strength is made perfect in weakness, we thank you for the unseen ministries of children and young people, for your Spirit's work amongst them and for their impact upon the world today.

Show us again, how to come to you as Children.

OUTSIDERS IV (Refugees)

Loving God,
 We worship you as one whose own son was a refugee;
 We worship you as the God whose people fled slavery in Egypt,
 We worship you as the God whose people were dragged into captivity in Babylon.
 And we pray for those today who have fled their homes and their loved ones.
 Through hardship...
 Through disaster...
 Through persecution...
 Through war...
 Loving God, for those whose hearts are as broken as their homes; whose hope has all gone; who find themselves unwelcome wherever they seek help – show compassion.
 Show it through us.
 Show us what real hospitality looks like when it is a gift.
 Teach us how to welcome the stranger in our personal lives

and our politics.

Let the glory of your love break through your church and into the structures that govern our society.

OUTSIDERS V (Refugees II)

God of Exodus and Exile, we worship you as the God of displaced and oppressed peoples. We worship you as the one who lived as a refugee, in radical insecurity, as the God of heaven who – in Christ – had nowhere to lay his head.

Grant that our sense of the world might stretch beyond the institutionalised fantasy worldviews we have come to treasure. May our knowledge of the world reach beyond the limits of where media points us – that we might see a world where living in a steel container is luxury, where risking your life to find refuge in another country is the best option, where suicide feels like a reasonable response to personal disaster.

Give us the courage to see the world as it is – and to have a realistic sense of our own agency and power and responsibilities in that world:

Forgive us for seeing only the immediate crisis and not the Social totality. Open our eyes to the wider context that creates refugees, and of our complicity with forces that create refugees.

Forgive us for judging whether another human being deserves to be one of us, according only to their merits or their failures. Instead help us to see clearly sheer value of their shared humanity.

Forgive us for measuring others only by their economic status, their financial value, or their value to us. Help us to be a people who recognise the intrinsic value of everyone made in your image.

Forgive us for reducing human beings to numbers, demoting others from homo-sapiens, to homo-economicus, for dehumanising others

You are the God whose being finds expression above all in the lives those of refugee status – so help us to ditch our liturgical fantasies and worship you as you really are.

PERSONHOOD I (The Body)

Lord God, we worship you as Lord of heaven and earth, whose reach extends beyond the furthest galaxy, and into the depths of the human psyche.

We praise you as the word become flesh, the joy of heaven to earth come down. And so we thank you for the comforts we enjoy, the luxuries we might too readily take for granted, and the bodily pleasures that are gifts from you.

But we seek your help in becoming ever more fully human, ever more fully the people you have created us to be. When our shrink wrapped food distances us from all that was involved in providing us with a meal, awaken us to the world. To the consequences of our lifestyles on animals, on people, on our environment. And help us to learn the responsibilities that comfort brings.

When our central heating and double-glazing separates us from the seasons, from the rhythms of the world you have created, from the marvels of the world on our doorstep, and the beauty woven through the every day, awaken us again to our place in this world.

When our wardrobes fill with throwaway clothes – awaken

us to the plight of those who labour under terrible conditions to provide us with luxuries we don't need. Show us what it means to care for others, in such a way as to fight for changes in working conditions, for sustainable means of living.

We thank you for our place on this planet – and ask that you help us to become more attuned to one another, that we might become more attuned to you. That your word might become flesh in the way that we live from day to day, and that our lives might be living proof of your life-giving love.

PERSONHOOD II (Identity)

God of the cross, who calls us into a post-identity life, may our identity be truly rooted in you.

God of sameness and God of difference, we thank you for the complex networks of relationships and experiences that have shaped who we are today.

When our backgrounds and experiences have caused us damage and pain, we pray that you will bring us new experiences, new relationships and ways of relating, that may bring healing and change, without us losing who we really are in you.

And make us the means by which you might bring healing, and new experiences and new ways of relating to other people.

Where we look right through people whose lives do not register within the limits of our diversity, open our eyes afresh. That we might see those who have become invisible, speak with those who have been ignored, and hear those with no voice.

Where we consider others a threat to our treasured worldview – speak to us through those we may not want to hear, and show us how to listen.

Where the suffering of others does not attract our attention, where are care is limited to those with whom we identify, when our solidarity is selective – reveal yourself to us afresh as the cross-carrying deity. Who turns the world upside down.

We thank you for the complex networks that have formed us and shaped us, for the relationships we inhabit, and the opportunities of care that confront us – may we root our identity first and foremost, in you.

PERSONHOOD III (Alienation)

Lord God, we see you represented in the person of Jesus, we see your being, your power, your wisdom, all made present in the form of a powerless, peasant builder from nowhere town and with no influence, no wealth, no good reputation.

So show us what it means to represent you. To make you present in a world of power games, of trickle-up economics, of social fragmentation.

As we feel our world around us fragment into ever smaller groups of self-interest, as we become ever more suspicious and cynical about institutions that shape our daily living. May our living together, our interactions, our functioning as a community, reveal something better – may our life together, manifest something of a goodness, and a beauty that transcends our context.

As we see the plight of [victims of natural disaster], show us as a members of a wealthy democracy what representation looks like in a time of crisis. Show us how to be just with the resources you have put at our disposal – show us what it means to be present despite the distance of the suffering.

As we feel all too deeply the losses in our own community, we pray for those from within this community who are currently grieving, or alone, or immobile, or ill. May our words and our actions find themselves becoming a bridge for your presence, your company, your support.

May we be drawn to reflect on what we do with those few years that are given to us, so that we might re-present something bigger, greater than ourselves.

By your grace, show your church afresh – just what it means to represent you.

PERSONHOOD IV (Inclusivity and Diversity)

God of heaven and earth,

It infuriates us that you bless those with whom we disagree.

It irritates us that you love those we do not.

It angers us that you embrace those we would reject.

And we shudder to think you are a God of holiness. A God of difference, you reveal yourself as the Other.

God of inclusivity, you became human in the form of the outsider, the stranger and the misfit.

God of diversity, you know what it is to be excluded, rejected, slandered, and persecuted.

And so we pray that you alert us to our own blind spots.

Forgive us for assuming we have no blind spots.

And show us what it means to stop, to become attuned to you and our world.

And so today, we pray for our enemies. For those we have been trained to hate.

We think in particular, of members of political parties that offend us.

We pray for nations that we have been trained to fear, economically and militarily.

And now, we think of one person who we dislike, or who has hurt us. Bless them we pray. Help us to see your image reflected in them.

And by your grace, may your image be reflected in us as individuals and as a community. We thank you for this college, and the constant efforts and energies invested in being a welcoming community. Show us what it means to play our part. To remain alert to how others perceive us. And to remain true to spirit of openness, and inclusivity and diversity. Grant us the courage always to foster these qualities.

And may your beauty be reflected in our living and studying and working together.

SILENCE (Ps 19/46 / Luke 5:12-16)

We worship you as an active, world-making, world-changing God. And yet you invite us to encounter you in the stillness. And you call us to listen, to hear the other, in stillness. So may our stillness be a gift from you, and by your grace, may our stillness become a gift to the world.

When nations ramp up tensions against one another, when governments and media outlets seem to feed the hysteria and breathe out rumours of war, show us what it means to be still. To be actively still in a world-changing way.

When the pandemic forces stillness upon us, when being still means isolation, and loneliness and inactivity, show us a stillness that allows room for presence. For the presence of the other to connect with us. Show us what it means to bring a fruitful stillness to those who are isolated.

When being still is not quite still. When our relaxation is accompanied by the white noise of digital devices that invade our rest. When our smart-phones reduce us to unreflective docility. When our obedience to screens enmeshes us ever-more fully in a plate-spinning whirligig hyperactivity, teach us to be still. Genuinely still.

When nature itself becomes our sock-puppet. When we use it solely as a service-provider to reduce our stress, and refuse to allow its many voices to address us, show us what it means to be still.

As a people. As individuals. Show us when and how to shut up. Sit down. Be still. To the glory of your name.

TECHNOLOGY I (War)

Lord of heaven and earth,

Whose creative spirit animates human creativity.

Help us to use our minds to serve humanity rather than to destroy it. To humanise rather than dehumanize.

We pray for nations subjected to war, who have seen at close hand the devastating impact of human technologies. Whose homeland has become a magnet to military technologies that wreck human lives.

And we pray for nations who wage war, many of whose convictions and experiences are drowned out by their own government as well as ours, and by social media technologies that police human expression.

We pray for technologies that will no longer dehumanise

people into body counts and mortality rates. For medical technologies that promote health, that bring healing but threaten profits. That medical therapies will not be hindered by the profiteering of corporate giants.

And we pray for our own government in the coming days. Knowing that technologies cannot transform wilful stupidity into wisdom. We pray for political decision-making that considers the wellbeing of all people rather than the wealth of the few, the stability of a nation over the survival of powered interests. For decisions that do not treat human beings like human resources.

God of creation and creativity. Help us to use the gifts you have given us to the benefit of all, and to the glory of your name.

TECHNOLOGY II (Machine Intelligence and Creativity)

God of creation and creativity, we pray for the world you have created.
  When our intelligence is artificial,
  Alert us to our true goals, and purposes and objectives.
  When our personal opinions have been spoon fed to us,
  Give us the gift of discernment.
  When our self-styled dissent is manufactured,
  Show us how to listen well.
  When our compassion is automated,
  Give us the courage to feel as well as say the right thing.
  Where our individuality is mass-produced,
  Alert us to the cold realities of our world.
  Where others can lip-synch to our spontaneity,
  Give us the guts to unlearn as well as to learn.

Where our identity leads us to self-obsession,

Help us to welcome the stranger, engage the outsider, and to hear those we fear.

Where purple prose is mistaken for literature,

Awaken us to the holy, the other, the universe beyond our knowing.

Where multi-sensory titillation passes for art,

Show us how to use our senses and gifts, to experience and to work for liberation.

Where neoliberal platitude passes for poetry,

Show us how language can both stifle communication, and bring about justice.

In the world you have created, show us what it means for our creativity to mirror yours.

TECHNOLOGY III (Nervous Systems)

We worship you as a species who, for a nano-fragment of time, have taken the form of carnal matter.

When we gaze through a telescope or through a microscope, it seems astonishing humanity exists at all. That there is such thing as Life itself. And we marvel at the monstrous improbability of life ever having come about in the first place. The unacknowledged, and still underappreciated fragility of each life. And the very real prospect that, as a species, we are hell bent on microwaving ourselves out of existence.

As our world leaders gather to legislate on the survival of our species,

awaken us and them to our collective responsibilities.

Awaken us to the networks in which we find our place, the

relationships that – for better or worse – shape our identity.

As we reflect on the fact that this may be the only planet in our galaxy that currently sustains life, awaken us to the cosmic consequences of our down to earth actions. The galactic significance of our mundane and daily humdrum.

Awaken us to the complexities, the rootedness, of our life alongside other lives.

The responsibilities that come with being a human being with a brain and a voice.

Thank you, for the gifts each of us have received. And may we use those gifts in a way that affirms life, enables other to flourish, and brings glory to your name.

UNKNOWN GOD

God of heaven and earth,

Lord of the world we know, and the world beyond our knowing.

Show us what it means to be humble in light of what we do not know, or do not understand.

Grant us the capacity to be changed, surprised, transformed by that which we have feared, or doubted or detested.

Grant us the ability to sacrifice our certainties, for the sake of encountering the other, a person of whom we are suspicious, an idea we have not fully understood, a conviction or belief we have long assumed.

Grant us the readiness to change our minds when confronted with evidence.

Forgive us, when we allow our fear to disable us.

When we fear a difficult conversation so much, that we never have it.

When we surround ourselves with those who agree with us, and will confirm and strengthen us in all bias and prejudice.

When we are afraid to offer support, or offer an apology, help us to see our fears are usually far greater than the realities.

When we don't know what to say to those who need our help, give us the courage to inhabit their silence. To listen.

When we take the easy way out, because listening to another can disturb us to our core, make us healthily uncomfortable.

May we grow in our walk with you, in our relationships with one another.

That our lives and relationships and our listening, draw us and others into something bigger than ourselves.

To the glory of your name.

Printed in Great Britain
by Amazon

27158201R00116